TRACING [illegible]
OXFORDSHIRE
ANCESTORS

A Guide for Family and Local Historians

Nicola Lisle

First published in Great Britain in 2018
PEN & SWORD FAMILY HISTORY
an imprint of
Pen & Sword Books Ltd
47 Church Street, Barnsley, South Yorkshire, S70 2AS

ISBN 978 1 52672 3 956

A CIP catalogue record for this book is
available from the British Library.

Typeset in Palatino and Optima by CHIC GRAPHICS

Printed and bound in England by CPI Group (UK), Croydon, CR0 4YY

Pen & Sword Books Ltd incorporates the imprints of Pen & Sword
Airworld, Archaeology, Atlas, Aviation, Battleground, Discovery, Family
History, Fiction, History, Maritime, Military, Military Classics, Politics,
Select, Social History, True Crime, Frontline Books, Leo Cooper,
Remember When, Seaforth Publishing, The Praetorian Press,
Wharncliffe Local History, Wharncliffe Transport,
Wharncliffe True Crime and White Owl.

For a complete list of Pen & Sword titles please contact

PEN & SWORD BOOKS LTD
47 Church Street, Barnsley, South Yorkshire, S70 2AS, England
E-mail: enquiries@pen-and-sword.co.uk
Website: www.pen-and-sword.co.uk
or
PEN & SWORD BOOKS LTD
1950 Lawrence Rd., Havertown, PA 19083, USA
E-mail: Uspen-and-sword@casematepublishers.com
Website: www.penandswordbooks.com

CONTENTS

ACKNOWLEDGEMENTS

I would like to thank several people who have helped to make this book possible, including Helen Drury, Photographic and Oral History Officer at Oxfordshire History Centre, and other members of OHC staff; Anne Brunner-Ellis, Head of Design and Publications, Oxford University Images; Colin Harris, until recently the Superintendent at the Bodleian Library Special Collections Reading Rooms and a founder member of the Oxfordshire Family History Society; Alice Millea, Assistant Keeper of the Oxford University Archives; Dr Martin Maw, Archivist at Oxford University Press; Chelsea Eves, Assistant Curator at the River and Rowing Museum, Henley-on-Thames; Lauren Meehan, former Press and Marketing Officer at Oxford Playhouse; Dáire Rooney, Assistant Librarian at the Manuscripts and Archives Research Library, Trinity College, Dublin; and everyone else who has chipped in with useful bits of advice and information.

The front cover illustrations are of John Radcliffe, physician (1650–1714) by Sir Godfrey Kneller (1646–1723), 1712 © Oxford University Images/Bodleian Library, and the Witney Blanket Industry © Oxfordshire County Council, Oxford History Centre, all reproduced by kind permission.

Last but not least, I would like to thank my husband, James, and son, Ben, for their constant encouragement and support.

ABBREVIATIONS

BSP	Black Sheep Productions
BFHS	Berkshire Family History Society
BMD	Birth, marriage and death indexes/certificates
BNA	British Newspaper Archive
BOD	Bodleian Library Special Collections
BRO	Berkshire Record Office
CBS	Centre for Buckinghamshire Studies
EP	Eureka Partnership
FFHS	Federation of Family History Societies
GRO	General Register Office
MRC	Modern Records Centre (University of Warwick)
OBUSC	Oxford Brookes University Special Collections
OCL	Oxfordshire County Library
OHA	Oxfordshire Health Archives
OHC	Oxfordshire History Centre
OUA	Oxford University Archives
OUP	Oxford University Press Archives & Museum
PA	Parliamentary Archives
SOFO	Soldiers of Oxfordshire Museum & Archives
SoG	Society of Genealogists
TNA	The National Archives
UBTC	University of Bristol Theatre Collection
TAPC	V&A Museum Theatre and Performance Collections

Chapter 1

INTRODUCTION TO OXFORDSHIRE

Oxfordshire is a gloriously diverse county, both geographically and historically. It shares borders with six other counties – Berkshire, Buckinghamshire, Gloucestershire, Northamptonshire, Warwickshire and Wiltshire – and encompasses the chalk landscape of the Vale of White Horse and the Chilterns to the south and the east, the distinctive limestone plateau of the Cotswolds to the west and gently rolling hills to the north. With its nature-rich pastures and woodlands, ancient remains and network of canals and rivers, interspersed with sleepy villages and historic market towns, it is arguably one of our most quintessentially English counties.

Before the reorganisation of the counties in 1974, much of southern Oxfordshire was in Berkshire, with the River Thames forming a natural boundary.

A traditionally agricultural county, Oxfordshire relied on the land for its livelihood for centuries. The Cotswold sheep spawned a thriving wool trade from around the thirteenth century, with the tiny market town of Witney becoming the centre of a world-famous blanket industry. Other notable industries included glove-making, tanning, brewing, malting, rope-making, timber production and pottery.

It was not until the early twentieth century that Oxfordshire gained its first major non-agricultural industry with the founding of Morris Motors in Oxford in 1912. Morris revolutionised motoring in Britain by mass-producing affordable and reliable cars, and became the world's second-largest car manufacturer after Henry Ford.

Oxford University dates back to the late eleventh century and has nurtured many of England's notable men and women, from politicians and religious leaders to scientists, philosophers, writers, artists and sporting heroes, all of whom have left their imprint on the county's heritage. These include writers such as John Betjeman, Lewis Carroll, C.S. Lewis, J.R.R. Tolkien and Evelyn Waugh, astronomer Edmund Halley, explorer and writer T.E. Lawrence, architect Sir Christopher Wren, former prime ministers Margaret Thatcher, Edward Heath and Tony Blair, and many more.

A BRIEF HISTORY OF OXFORDSHIRE

Oxfordshire was first recognised as a county in 1007, but there is evidence of settlement in the area stretching back to the Ice Age. Roman occupation appears to have been sparse compared with other parts of the British Isles, but pottery remains have been found in and around the Oxford area, and in 1813 the mosaic floor of a Roman villa was uncovered at North Leigh in the west of the county.

Saxon tribes invaded the Thames Valley from the sixth century, and during the seventh century St Birinus brought Christianity to the area when he was appointed Bishop of Dorchester. By this time a significant settlement was beginning to form around the Thames between the two Anglo-Saxon kingdoms of Wessex and Mercia. Known as *Oxenforda* ('ford for oxen') – later Oxford – this was the site chosen by St Frideswide, a Mercian princess, to establish a monastery in around AD700. Legend has it that an unwanted suitor was struck blind when he pursued her to Oxford, but she took pity on him and restored his sight with water from the Holy Well at nearby Binsey. This story is immortalised in a stained-glass window in Christ Church Cathedral, which stands on the site of the original monastery.

In 1002, Oxford's 1,000-strong Danish population sought sanctuary in St Frideswide's monastery after Ethelred the Unready ordered the massacre of all Danish settlers in England. Their hiding place was quickly discovered and the building razed to the ground.

Seven years later, the Danes exacted revenge by ransacking the town, which was completely destroyed.

By the time of the Norman Conquest a new settlement had emerged and had developed into one of the largest towns in England. Robert d'Oilly established castles at Oxford and Wallingford, on the orders of William the Conqueror, and both of these were vital strongholds during the Norman occupation and during the English civil wars.

Royal Oxfordshire

Oxfordshire has a strong royal history. During the Anglo-Saxon period, there were royal manors at Bampton, Bloxham, Benson, Headington, Kirtlington, Shipton-under-Wychwood and Wootton, as well as royal forests at Bernwood, Shotover and Wychwood.

Oxford Castle was built after the Norman Conquest. © Nicola Lisle

Henry I enclosed Woodstock Park in 1129 and built a hunting lodge there. The following year he built Beaumont Palace in Oxford, just outside the city's north gate, and two future kings, both sons of Henry II, were born there: Richard the Lionheart in 1157 and John in 1167.

Henry II established a royal palace at Woodstock, where he famously wooed his mistress, Rosamund Clifford ('Fair Rosamund'), and granted the town a Royal Charter in 1179. Woodstock Palace continued to be used by successive kings until the building was destroyed during the English Civil War. After lying derelict for sixty years, the land was cleared to make way for Blenheim Palace, which was built for John Churchill, the first Duke of Marlborough, as a monument to his momentous and decisive victory at the Battle of Blenheim in 1704.

Henry II's succession to the throne came about as the result of a civil war between King Stephen and his cousin, Empress Matilda. In 1142, during the Anarchy (1135–53), Empress Matilda thwarted her cousin by escaping from Oxford Castle and making her way across the frozen Thames to Wallingford, dressed entirely in white so that she was invisible against the snow and ice. The Anarchy ended with the Treaty of Wallingford in 1153, which forced Stephen to recognise Matilda's son, Henry, as his rightful heir. When he became king in 1154, Henry II rewarded Wallingford for its loyalty by granting it a Royal Charter the following year.

During the English Civil War (1642–51), Oxford was the Royalist capital of England, with Charles I establishing his court and military headquarters there after the Parliamentarians forced him to flee London in 1642. For the next four years, Royalist soldiers were billeted around the town, a Royal Mint was established, domestic properties were ruthlessly destroyed to make way for defensive earthworks and Oxford Castle became a prison for captured Parliamentarians. Royalist soldiers also captured Broughton Castle, near Banbury, after the Battle of Edgehill in 1642, causing extensive damage to the building. The war ended in 1646 when both Oxford and Wallingford castles were forced to surrender to Cromwell's armies. Wallingford Castle was virtually destroyed, but Oxford Castle continued to be used as a prison until as recently as 1996.

In the aftermath of the Civil War, rebel Parliamentarians began agitating for greater social equality and religious tolerance, which Cromwell was not prepared to consider. The rebels, known as the Levellers, led a mutiny in the spring of 1649, marching from Salisbury to Banbury and on to Burford, where they were overwhelmed by Cromwell's forces and around 300 of the rebels were imprisoned in Burford Church. One of them, Anthony Sedley, carved his name into the font accompanied by the words '1649, prisner' [sic]. Three of the Levellers – Cornet Thompson, Corporal Perkins and Private Church – were shot in the churchyard on 17 May 1649 as an example to the other mutineers. Burford now holds an annual Levellers Day to mark this event.

The founding of the university

While much of Oxford's expansion as a town was due to its importance as a royal stronghold, it also owes its growth to the founding of the university. Established in the eleventh century as a centre of learning for the clergy, it developed rapidly and by the thirteenth century was attracting various orders of monks and friars to the town, as well as enjoying royal and episcopal patronage.

Inevitably, the increasing power and privileges enjoyed by the university caused local resentment. Tensions between 'town and gown' were rife in medieval Oxford and frequently erupted into violence. The most notorious incident was the St Scholastica's Day riot of 1355, which began as a minor skirmish but quickly escalated into a three-day conflict that saw university buildings vandalised and some of the clerics allegedly killed. As a result, some of the town's administration was handed to the university, a situation not reversed until the nineteenth century.

Nevertheless, the university was a welcome source of prosperity for the town and its surrounding towns and villages, as local tradesmen and craftsmen benefitted from the increased population.

Towards modern Oxfordshire

The construction of the Oxford Canal in the late eighteenth century and the coming of the railway in the mid-nineteenth century brought the first stirrings of modernisation to what was still a largely agricultural county. Oxford and the hitherto insignificant village of Didcot were transformed by the establishment of railway junctions, while Banbury became a bustling canal-side town.

Non-agricultural industries began to appear, notably William Carter's ironworks in Oxford in 1812 and Bernard Samuelson's pioneering agricultural engineering firm in Banbury in 1848. Oxfordshire breweries flourished during the eighteenth and nineteenth centuries. All this paved the way for greater industrialisation in the county, and it arrived at the turn of the twentieth century in the form of the Morris Motors car factory, which changed the character and economic fabric of Oxford forever.

As agricultural industries declined during the twentieth century, others took over. Car production is now in the hands of BMW, which has been producing the new Mini in Oxford since 2001. Oxford University Press, which was established in the seventeenth century, is now a major international publishing house. Other important industries include tourism, retail, finance, hi-tech industries and scientific research.

THE ORGANISATION OF THE COUNTY

Our local government structure is a complicated one that has evolved over hundreds of years. It was not until the Local Government Act of 1888 that a universal system was introduced in England and Wales, with further reforms being introduced in subsequent Acts – the most radical of which was the county boundary changes that were introduced in 1974. For anyone researching family history, it is helpful to have a knowledge of the different units of local government over the centuries, what kind of records they generated and how these can help you with your research.

Historic counties

The earliest county boundaries were based on the Anglo-Saxon kingdoms and shires. From around the tenth century, southern counties were subdivided into hundreds, each hundred having its own court and responsibility for judicial proceedings and administration. In the Danelaw counties – mostly those in the north, East Anglia and the south-eastern Midlands – these administrative divisions were known as wapentakes.

Oxfordshire's hundreds included Bampton, Banbury, Binfield, Bloxham, Bullingdon, Chadlington, Dorchester, Ewelme, Kirtlington, Langtree, Lewknor, Oxford City and University, Oxford City, Oxford Liberty, Pyrton, Ploughley, Thame and Wootton. The Kirtlington hundred was absorbed into the Ploughley hundred in the twelfth century.

Within these hundreds lay individual parishes, which evolved from the ancient manors and townships. The evolution wasn't an organised one; boundaries of parishes and townships didn't always coincide, and sometimes one township would contain two parishes. Some towns existed outside parish boundaries and were known as extra-parochial towns.

In the sixteenth century the parish was adopted as the main unit of local governance, signalling the gradual breaking away from the system of manorial jurisdiction. From 1538, baptisms, marriages and burials were recorded in parish registers, and these are now an important source for family historians. Parishes also became officially responsible for law and order, collecting local and national taxes, maintaining the highways and looking after the poor.

Boroughs

From the Middle Ages, large towns and cities were granted the right to become self-governing, a privilege that was conferred by Royal Charter. The boroughs were run by corporations, which typically included a mayor, aldermen and burgesses, often with links to local merchants' guilds and manorial estates. Boroughs could hold markets and fairs, set local levies, lease property, pass bye-laws, regulate sanitary laws and form their own courts of justice. From the thirteenth century, boroughs had two representatives in Parliament, and the later Parliamentary constituencies were based on the old borough boundaries.

When boroughs were abolished in 1974 as part of the county boundary shake-up, Oxfordshire had four surviving boroughs. These, with their charter dates, were: Woodstock (1453), Banbury (1554), Chipping Norton (1606) and Henley (1722).

Borough archives are held at the OHC in series BOR1-BOR4, and include such things as charters and other founding documents, council papers, judicial records, property and financial records, rent books, apprenticeship registers and much more.

Quarter Sessions

From 1361, counties and county boroughs had their own courts, presided over by Justices of the Peace, who tried petty crimes, settled local disputes, ensured religious conformity, regulated trade, employment and apprenticeships, looked after the poor and oversaw the administrative and maintenance responsibilities of the parishes that fell within their jurisdiction. The Quarter Sessions were so named because they convened on quarter days, roughly three months apart. Quarter Sessions and the Courts of Assize – which tried capital and other serious offences – were replaced with the Crown Court in 1972.

The Quarter Sessions produced a vast quantity of records and these are a valuable resource for family historians, particularly in relation to crime and the Poor Law. The Oxfordshire records cover the pre-1974 county and are held at the OHC in series QS1831-QS1857. Most of the catalogue can only be viewed on index cards in the searchroom, but some post-1830 records are searchable online. An eleven-volume set of records compiled by Canon Oldfield in the early 20th century has been digitised and put on DVD by the OFHS, and this is available for purchase through the Society or at the OHC.

Local Government in the Nineteenth Century

County councils and county boroughs were established in England and Wales on 1 April 1889 by the Local Government Act 1888, and took over the administrative functions of the Quarter Sessions. A further Act in 1894 sub-divided the county councils into urban and rural district councils, which largely took over from the sanitary districts introduced in 1875 and were responsible for public health issues. Parish councils were also introduced to take over from the old ecclesiastical parishes. County councils and their subdivisions were known as administrative counties.

Oxford City was a county borough from 1889 until the county boroughs were abolished in 1974. Records are held at OHC in the Oxford City Archive (OCA) and are only available in the searchroom.

Oxfordshire's urban district councils from 1894 until their abolition in 1974 were: Bicester, Caversham (until 1911, when it became part of Reading County Borough in Berkshire), Thame, Wheatley and Witney. Rural district councils were Banbury (1894–1974), Bicester (1894–1932), Bullingdon (1932–1974), Chipping Norton (1894-1974), Crowmarsh (1894–1932), Culham (1894–1932), Goring (1894–1932), Headington (1894–1932), Henley (1894–1974), Ploughley (1932–1974), Thame (1894–1932), Witney (1894–1974) and Woodstock (1894–1932). Records for district councils are held at the OHC in the UDC and RDC series. The OHC also has downloadable fact sheets for boroughs and district councils, which can be found under 'Running the county' in the 'Archives and collections' section.

County boundary changes of 1974

The Local Government Act 1972, which came into effect in England and Wales on 1 April 1974, introduced major changes to the local authority system and redefined county boundaries. Oxfordshire gained the North Berkshire towns of Abingdon, Didcot, Faringdon, Wallingford and Wantage – the records for which are still with the BRO – Caversham had already been lost to Berkshire in 1911 and Stokenchurch to Buckinghamshire in 1896.

Oxfordshire gained the town of Abingdon in 1974. © Nicola Lisle

Five new district councils were created in Oxfordshire in 1974: Cherwell, Oxford City, Vale of White Horse, West Oxfordshire and South Oxfordshire. The Vale of White Horse District Council largely encompasses the former Berkshire rural district councils of Abingdon, Faringdon, Wallingford and Wantage, as well as Wantage Urban District Council.

Oxfordshire became a ceremonial county, or lieutenancy, when ceremonial counties were created by the Local Government Act 1997.

OVERVIEW OF OXFORDSHIRE'S ARCHIVES AND RESOURCES

Oxfordshire is richly endowed with general and specialist archives, which will be explored in more detail in the following chapters. This summary will help to give an overview of the most essential resources. Full contact details are given in the directory at the back of this book.

Oxfordshire History Centre

The OHC (www.oxfordshire.gov.uk/cms/public-site/oxfordshire-history-centre) is the main county archive, and contains all the holdings from the former Oxfordshire Record Office and the Oxfordshire Health Archives. The collection includes census returns, civil and parish registers, non-conformist records, court and police records, school admission records, electoral registers, wills, local government records, maps, newspapers and periodicals, books and pamphlets, street and trade directories, photographs, oral history recordings and deposited papers by local families, individuals, businesses, clubs and societies.

Find the records you are interested in by using their online Heritage Search facility (www.oxfordshire.gov.uk/heritagesearch), then quote the reference numbers to view original documents when you visit the Centre. It is advisable to book a space in the searchroom as it does sometimes get busy. You will need a County Archive Research Network (CARN) ticket to use the Reading Room, and you can obtain this on the day of your first visit on production of two passport-size photographs and some form of ID (e.g. driving licence, passport, utility bill). The ticket is free, and can be used at other public libraries. Note that many of the early catalogues are only available on card indexes in the OHC searchroom.

If you are unable to visit the Centre there is a research service, for which a fee is charged.

The Oxfordshire History Centre is based in the former St Luke's Church in Cowley, which is well served by local buses. Alternatively, there are several large car parks approximately five minutes' walk away. There is a café on site, free wi-fi and disabled access.

Oxfordshire County Library

Recently refurbished as part of Oxford's Westgate development, Oxfordshire County Library (formerly Oxford Central Library) is another great resource for family historians. The top floor (accessible by stairs and lift) has extensive Local History and Family History sections. Of particular interest is the series of booklets by Oxfordshire Black Sheep Publications, which includes transcriptions of coroners' inquests, police recruitment registers and minute books, bastardy trials and Poor Law Union and workhouse records.

Smaller stocks of local and family history books can also be found at other county libraries.

Computers at all the county libraries can be used to access Ancestry and Findmypast free of charge. These websites are also available to access at home through Reference Online (see below).

For more information about library services and to find individual libraries, visit www.oxfordshire.gov.uk/cms/public-site/libraries.

Reference Online

Available to all holders of an Oxfordshire library card, Reference Online (https://www.oxfordshire.gov.uk/cms/public-site/reference-online) gives access to a wide range of general reference works such as the *Oxford Dictionary of National Biography*, *Who's Who* and *Who Was Who*, leading family history websites Ancestry (Library Edition) and Findmypast, and various newspaper archives including the British Library Newspapers Collection, British Newspapers Archive, John Johnson Collection, Newsquest Digital Newspaper Archive and *The Times* Digital Archive 1785–2011. Note that some of the newspaper collections are accessible in libraries only, while others can be accessed at home. To find out more about Oxfordshire library membership, visit https://www.oxfordshire.gov.uk/cms/content/join-library.

Oxfordshire Family History Society

The OFHS (www.ofhs.org.uk) has produced a range of transcripts covering Oxfordshire and North Berkshire, including parish and non-conformist registers, college registers, census indexes, wills and memorial inscriptions. All of these are available to buy on CD or view free at Oxfordshire History Centre and Oxfordshire County Library (see above). You can also view Honour Rolls from both world wars on the society's website. These are listed alphabetically by surname and give details of a person's regiment, how they died and date of death.

If you need advice with a specific problem, the society runs regular help desks at the Oxfordshire History Centre and at Oxfordshire libraries. Check the website for locations, dates and times, and note that some need to be booked in advance. The society also holds monthly talks (open to non-members), produces a members-only journal three times a year and has its own annual family history fair.

Weston Library, Oxford, which opened in 2015 and now houses the Bodleian Library's Special Collections. © Nicola Lisle

In 2017, the OFHS launched a two-year project to compile a database of Oxfordshire surnames gleaned from local parish registers from 1538. Some of the results of their research are on their website, with others being added as the project progresses. This will enable family historians to find out about the origins and locations of their family surname.

The EurekA Partnership

The EurekA Partnership has transcribed and published a range of useful records for family historians, and these are available to purchase from their website: www.eurekapartnership.com. Oxfordshire titles include transcriptions of non-conformist records, marriage notices, probate notices, canal boat records and registers, a range of records relating to specific towns in the 'People Of' series, and miscellaneous records.

Bodleian Library

The Bodleian Library Special Collections and the Oxford University Archive between them hold student and staff records as well as papers relating to university clubs, societies and associations, official university magazines and deposited papers relating to individuals.

Oxford University was responsible for the administration of Oxford City from the fourteenth century to the mid-nineteenth century, and the Bodleian Library still holds many of the records that you would normally expect to find in the local record office. This includes poll books, Oxfordshire deeds, calendar of charters and rolls, prints and photographs, books, maps, estate records, diaries, topographical collections and other miscellaneous papers and collections. See details of their holdings at http://ox.libguides.com/modern-sc/ collections. Special Collections also includes the John Johnson Collection, a vast collection of printed ephemera. You will need a Bodleian Library Reader's Ticket to access the collections; details are on the website (www.bodleian.ox.ac.uk/using/getting-a-readers-card).

Berkshire Record Office

Records relating to the towns and districts that were part of Berkshire before 1974 are still held at the Berkshire Record Office (www.berkshirerecordoffice.org.uk). As might be expected, holdings include parish and other registers, wills and probate records, electoral registers and poll books, BMD (birth, marriage and death) indexes, census returns and more. The BRO also offers free access to Ancestry and Findmypast.

OTHER ARCHIVES

As well as local archives, you will almost certainly need to broaden your searches to national repositories and to make use of online resources. Some of the most useful are detailed below.

The National Archives

The National Archives at Kew is one of the largest repositories in the UK, and an essential resource for any family research. The main website at www.nationalarchives.gov.uk has links to a wide range of research guides (searchable by subject or by alphabetical listing), and to their online Discovery catalogue (http://discovery.nationalarchives.gov.uk). If you need some help getting started, click on 'Help with your research', then on the next screen click on

'Unfamiliar with archives?'. This will give you useful pointers about what records they hold and what they don't hold, which records are available online and which are not. As with the OHC, you will need a reader's ticket to view original documents, but not to view documents on microfilm and microfiche.

The former Access to Archives (A2A) website and National Register of Archives Index have now been incorporated into the Discovery catalogue.

Parliamentary Archives

The Parliamentary Archives – which comprises collections from both Houses of Parliament – is a rich source of information, encompassing records related to divorce, name changes and naturalisation, judicial records, Roman Catholic and Protestation returns, petitions to parliament, private bills, deposited plans and government reports. The website (www.parliament.uk/archives) gives a good overview of the archive with useful links, including to its catalogue Portcullis (www.portcullis.parliament.uk/calmview). A good place to start is the 'Family History at the Parliamentary Archives' link in the 'Explore' section.

The Modern Records Centre, University of Warwick

This is the principal repository for archives relating to trade unions, employers' organisations, trade associations, pressure and protest groups, political groups, transport organisations and various individuals associated with any of the above. The website (https://warwick.ac.uk/services/library/mrc) gives details of its holdings as well as providing various research guides. The family history research guide includes a handy list of trades and occupations, each of which links to a page giving information about relevant MRC holdings and where to find further information.

Society of Genealogists

Founded in 1911, the Society of Genealogists (www.sog.org.uk) is the UK's largest and most comprehensive source of family history information, including many unique collections. You can search the library catalogue and surname index online, while the 'Learn' section has downloadable guides and a series of hints and tips. Anyone can visit the library, but non-members need hourly or daily passes. The website gives details of membership benefits and how to join. The society also runs free library tours as well as a range of regular events including study days, workshops, lectures, walks and conferences.

Useful websites

The largest online collection of family history records is Family Search (www.familysearch.org), which is provided by the Church of Jesus Christ of Latter-Day Saints and offers free access. There are many more free websites and online forums, full details of which are given in the directory at the back of this book.

The two main subscription sites are Ancestry (www.ancestry.co.uk) and Findmypast (www.findmypast.co.uk). Both offer fourteen-day free trials and occasionally free access to a specific collection of records for a limited period. There are different levels of membership, so you can pick one that best suits your needs. You can also access these sites free at the OHC, Oxfordshire public libraries and TNA, or from home via Reference Online if you hold an Oxfordshire library card (see above).

HOW TO USE THIS BOOK

This book takes a detailed look at the archives available to family historians in Oxfordshire while also capturing some of the county's history so that you get a sense of the place in which your ancestors lived, worked and played. Whether you are a beginner or an experienced genealogist, I aim to introduce you to a wide range of resources and explain how they can help you in your family research.

The early chapters of this book deal with the essential building blocks of any family research – civil registration, census returns, parish registers and other primary sources. These help you to put names and dates on your family tree. The book then moves on to other sources that help you to delve more deeply into your ancestors' lives, fleshing out those facts and figures by finding out more about them as people and putting their lives into a historical and social context. Bear in mind, though, that all archives have restricted access for a set period, which varies from one archive to another. For some, the closure period is fifty years; for others, such as the census returns, it is 100 years.

Museums are a vital ingredient in discovering your ancestor's story as they can tell you a lot about local places, occupations, customs and traditions, all of which helped shape your ancestors' lives and those of successive generations. Oxfordshire is rich in museums, some of which have archives as well, so each chapter includes suggested places to visit to help bring your family story to life.

There is, of course, far more information about Oxfordshire's history and genealogy than can be contained within this book, so each chapter also includes suggestions for further reading and research.

To save repetition, I have used abbreviations for the main archives, and these are listed at the beginning of the book for easy reference.

Finally, there is a handy directory at the end of the book with a detailed listing of archives, museums and useful websites.

FURTHER READING

Graham, Malcolm, *Oxford Then and Now*, The History Press, 2011
Hey, David, *The Oxford Companion to Local and Family History*, OUP, 2001 (reprint)
Jenkins, Stanley C., *Oxford History Tour*, Amberley Publishing, 2017
Jessup, Mary, *History of Oxfordshire*, Phillimore & Co Ltd, 1975
Koenig, Chris, *Oxford Past Times*, Signal Books, 2013
MacCannell, Daniel, *Oxford: Mapping the City*, Berlinn Ltd, 2016
Raymond, Stuart A., *Oxfordshire: A Genealogical Bibliography*, Federation of Family History Societies, 1993
Steane, John, *Oxfordshire*, Pimlico, 1996
Whitfield, Peter, *Oxford in Prints: 1675-1900*, The Bodleian Library, 2016

Chapter 2

GETTING STARTED WITH OXFORDSHIRE RECORDS

CIVIL REGISTRATION

Official registration of all births, marriages and deaths in England and Wales began on 1 July 1837, following the passing of the Marriages Act 1836 and the founding of the General Register Office (GRO). Although there are inevitably some inaccuracies, the birth, marriage and death (BMD) certificates and indexes are among the most reliable sources of information for family historians and are an ideal place to start your research.

England and Wales were divided into registration districts based on the old Poor Law Union boundaries (see Chapter 4). After the county boundary reorganisation of 1974, many of these original registration districts were either abolished or absorbed into other districts, so you might need to search neighbouring districts for your ancestors. You can find out more about the Oxfordshire registration districts here: www.ukbmd.org.uk/reg/oxf.html.

Local registrars were responsible for compiling indexes of births, marriages and deaths in their district and sending quarterly returns to the GRO, which then created a separate set of indexes. The GRO indexes list births, marriages and deaths in separate groups and were compiled quarterly until 1984, when they became annual. The quarterly indexes were arranged as follows:

- March quarter: January to March
- June quarter: April to June

- September quarter: July to September
- December quarter: October to December

The first index available is the one for September 1837.

Searching the BMD indexes

The Oxfordshire indexes to births, marriages and deaths are available for searching at the Oxfordshire Registration Service (www.oxfordshire.gov.uk/cms/public-site/births-deaths-and-ceremonies), for which a fee is payable. Copies of certificates can be ordered here: www.oxfordshire.gov.uk/cms/public-site/certificates-births-deaths-and-marriages.

Alternatively, you can search the indexes on the GRO website (www.gro.gov.uk/gro/content/certificates/Login.asp). You will need to create an account first, which is free. From here you will see links to family history advice, how to order certificates and more. Certificates currently cost £9.25. In October 2017, the GRO began piloting a service to provide birth certificates (1837–1916) and death certificates (1837–1957) as PDFs, at a cost of £6 each. Initially announced as a three-month pilot, at the time of writing this had been extended to a minimum of nine months.

You can also search the GRO indexes free at www.freebmd.org.uk, which covers the period 1837–1983 (although it is not yet complete), or use www.ancestry.co.uk or www.findmypast.com free of charge at the OHC or in one of the Oxfordshire libraries.

What the indexes and certificates tell you

All index entries include the GRO reference number, which you will need for ordering certificates, and the registration district. In addition, they include the following information:

- For births, the baby's full name (middle initials only from September 1911) and mother's maiden name (from September 1911)

- For marriages, the full names of the bride and bridegroom, listed individually (name of spouse included from March 1912)
- For deaths, full name of the deceased, age at death (date of birth from June 1969).

When searching the indexes, it is important to be aware that a lot of inaccuracies crept in, both at local level and when the information was being transcribed by the GRO. The most common mistakes are spellings, either because the transcriber misheard or because they deciphered someone's handwriting incorrectly. To save yourself the possibility of buying a certificate that turns out to be for the wrong person, try cross-referencing information to other ancestors.

Once you are certain enough of your search results to obtain certificates, you will have a wealth of useful details in your hands. These include:

Births
- Date and place of birth
- Child's full name and gender
- Name and surname of father (if this information is missing, the child was probably illegitimate)
- Mother's full name and maiden name (from 1969, place of birth)
- Father's occupation (mother's occupation included from 1984)
- Signature, description and residence of informant (usually the mother)
- Date of registration

Marriages
- Date of marriage
- Parish in which marriage took place
- Full names and ages of bride and groom
- Marital status (i.e. bachelor, spinster, widow, widower)
- Occupation (usually groom only)
- Places of residence at the time of marriage
- Names and occupations of fathers (it was announced in

December 2017 that mothers' details could soon be added to the digital registers)
- Whether the marriage was by banns or licence
- Signatures of bride, groom and two witnesses
- Name of the clergyman officiating at the ceremony

Deaths
- Date and place of death
- Full name of the deceased (from 1969, maiden name also included for married women)
- Gender
- Age at death (from March 1969 place and date of birth)
- Occupation and place of residence
- Name, address and signature of informant, and relationship to the deceased
- Cause of death and whether an inquest was held
- Date of registration
- Name and signature of registrar

All of this information is invaluable for establishing links with other family members or confirming existing details that you were unsure about. Family history research is a bit of a detective game, but the more details you discover, the more avenues of enquiry are opened up to you.

CENSUS RETURNS

National censuses have been carried out in Britain every ten years since 1801, and it is possible to glean all kinds of useful information from them. For each census, every household had to give details of all occupants of that address on a specific night, thereby preserving a fascinating snapshot of a family group captured at a precise moment in time. As well as giving us a window into our ancestors' world, the census returns can help to establish family relationships (from 1851), and confirm or supplement information from the BMD records.

Every household was required by law to complete a census form (also known as a 'schedule'). These details were then transferred into a book by the local enumerator and sent to the local authority for analysis. In most cases, it is the enumerators' books that have survived, not the original schedules. The exception is the 1911 census, for which both schedules and enumerators' books exist.

The earliest censuses were carried out by parish officials and their purpose was to assess the growth and make-up of the population in terms of age, gender and occupation. In 1841, the census was taken over by the General Register Office and administered using the new civil registration districts. From this point, the census returns started asking for an increasing amount of detail, so it is these later censuses that are of most use to family historians.

The information you can expect to find for each household in the census records includes:

- From 1841, each occupant's first name and surname, county of birth, profession or occupation, gender and age (rounded down to the nearest five for anyone aged fifteen and over);
- From 1851, each occupant's full name, age at last birthday, relationship to the head of the household, marital status, county and parish of birth (or country of birth if born outside England and Wales), and whether any member of the household suffered any disabilities;
- From 1891, employment status (i.e. employed, self-employed or unemployed), and number of rooms in the house if less than five;
- From 1901, number of people working from home;
- From 1911, the number of years a couple had been married, the number of children born alive and the number still living, type of property (e.g. house or flat), enumerator's route and local population statistics.

As with the GRO indexes, bear in mind that censuses are not wholly accurate, for a number of reasons. People often made mistakes on the census returns and some details are inconsistent from one census return to another. Many people were illiterate, and either guessed at answers or dictated to the enumerators, who may have then noted the details down incorrectly (particularly in the spellings of names). Enumerators also made mistakes if handwriting on the census returns was difficult to decipher. Some people lied about their details, either as a cover for illegal activity or because they objected to what they saw as an invasion of their privacy. Others (an estimated 5 per cent) were omitted from the censuses altogether, usually because they were travelling on the census night.

Despite all this, the censuses are a vital genealogical source that can give you some useful pointers for further research. The best way to approach the censuses is to treat information with caution, consult all the relevant censuses for each ancestor and verify details with other sources such as the civil registration records and parish registers (See Chapter 3).

Where to find census records

The censuses for 1841 to 1911 have all been fully indexed and can be searched online or viewed in person at archives and libraries. Censuses are only open to the public after 100 years, so at the time of writing the 1911 census is the latest one available. The 1921 census will be available in 2022.

The OHC has images, transcripts and indexes of census returns from 1841 onwards. These are not available online but can be viewed in the searchroom. Use Heritage Search for more information. The OFHS has enumerators' books and indexes for the 1841–1901 censuses available to purchase on CD (www.ofhs.org.uk/CDsales. html#censebs).

You can also view the censuses at TNA, or search the censuses free on Findmypast and Ancestry via their websites. There is a charge to view or download full transcriptions. TNA's guide to the census is very useful and includes the reference numbers and links to each census: www.nationalarchives.gov.uk/help-with-your-research/research -guides/census-records.

Finally, you can search and view transcripts free of charge at www.freecen.org.uk, but this doesn't currently include the 1911 census.

PROBATE RECORDS

Wills and other probate documents can be fertile hunting ground for the family historian, providing golden nuggets of information that you are unlikely to find anywhere else. The contents of a will can reveal details about some of the most intimate aspects of your ancestor's life, from treasured personal possessions and favourite charities, to the existence of illegitimate offspring or distant relations you may not have come across in the BMC and census records. The size of an estate, the court in which probate was granted and the nature of the bequests can tell you a lot about your ancestor's wealth, social status, lifestyle, interests, religion and political persuasion. This is where a 'real' picture of your ancestor can start to emerge.

Occasionally, family members that you might expect to find mentioned in a will are missing. This could indicate a rift in the family, or it might be that the deceased had already made private, unofficial bequests to certain members of the family, most likely a son or daughter. It could also mean that the missing person had already died by that date, which is useful if you have been unsure of someone's dates as it can help narrow down the possibilities.

Information in wills varies, but is likely to include the following:

- Deceased's full name, date of birth, place of residence and occupation;
- Names and addresses of beneficiaries, and their relationship to the deceased and to each other;
- Married names of any female members of the family, and the names of their spouses;
- Names and addresses of previously unknown family members or friends, such as an illegitimate child or a mistress;

- Names of executors and witnesses;
- Size and value of the estate;
- Place of burial or cremation;
- Date of probate (i.e. legally proving the will).

These can help you clarify existing details in your family tree and possibly enable you to add more names and dates.

Inventories

The executors of a will sometimes arranged for an inventory to be made of the deceased's possessions, usually to ensure fair distribution of property to beneficiaries and to prevent potential disputes. They were discontinued in the late eighteenth century. Oxfordshire inventories have survived for the period 1620–1710.

Administration bonds (Admons)

If a person died intestate, members of the family or other interested parties could apply to administer the estate. An Administration Bond (or Admon) was issued to ensure the work was carried out fairly. Admons are not as useful as wills and inventories for the family historian, but they can reveal some useful details about the deceased and their next of kin.

Probate before 1858

Before 1858, probate was the responsibility of the Church. Most wills were proved in the diocesan, archdeaconry or peculiar courts, depending on the value and location of properties owned. If the deceased held properties in more than one diocese, their probate was administered by one of the prerogative courts – for Oxfordshire, this was the Prerogative Court of Canterbury, which had jurisdiction over the south of England and Wales.

Oxfordshire wills date roughly from 1542, when the Diocese of Oxford was created, although a few have survived from as early as 1516. Probate records from the local ecclesiastical courts are held at the OHC, and you can search the collection online via Findmypast (https://search.findmypast.co.uk/search-word-Records/oxfordshire-wills-index-1516-1857). Access is free at the OHC.

The records are also listed in three volumes published by the British Record Society, covering the bishops' and archdeaconry courts for 1516–1732 and the peculiar courts from 1733–1857. Copies are available at the OHC and in major libraries.

The OFHS has transcribed the texts of wills and other probate documents, and you can search the records at www.wills.oxfordshire ghs.org.uk. The website includes some historical background, tips on searching and a handy glossary of unfamiliar words you are likely to come across in the transcriptions. There is also a CD available for purchase containing the Berkshire Probate Index for 1480–1857 (www.ofhs.org.uk/CDsales.html#brkprob).

The EP has published a series of booklets relating to Oxfordshire probate records, and these are available to purchase from their website: www.eurekapartnership.com.

Wills proved in the Prerogative Court of Canterbury 1383–1858 are held on microfilm at TNA, series PROB 11; see their search guide www.nationalarchives.gov.uk/help-with-your-research/research-guides/wills-1384-1858. TNA also has a general research guide at www.nationalarchives.gov.uk/help-with-your-research/research-guides/wills-or-administrations-before-1858.

The OUA holds wills of college fellows and other workers within the university, which were administered by the Chancellor's Court of the University of Oxford from 1436 until 1858. John Griffiths' *An Index to Wills Proved in the Court of the Chancellor of the University of Oxford* (OUP, 1862) is available online at https://books.google.co.uk/books?id=VYEHAAAAQAAJ.

Note that probate jurisdiction for Berkshire and Buckinghamshire was transferred to the Oxford diocese in 1836 and 1845 respectively. Most of these records are now held by the BRO and CBS, but there are a few within the Oxfordshire wills collection.

Probate from 1858

From 12 January 1858, responsibility for probate was transferred to a new civil Court of Probate, created by the Court of Probate Act 1857. A Principal Probate Registry was established in London, along with a network of district probate registries in England and Wales. Their website has an online search function as well as advice on searching and ordering copies: www.gov.uk/wills-probate-inheritance/searching-for-probate-records.

The National Probate Calendar (www.ancestry.co.uk/uk/probate) indexes have been published every year since 1858, and the records for 1973–95 have recently been added. Information included in the indexes includes:

- Date and place of death;
- Full names of executors and administrators;
- Date and place of probate;
- Value of the estate.

You can also view the Probate Calendar 1853–1943 on microfiche in the BOD (www.bodleian.ox.ac.uk/weston).

TNA also has a useful research guide at www.nationalarchives.gov.uk/help-with-your-research/research-guides/wills-or-administrations-after-1858/.

The EP has published several volumes of transcripts of Oxfordshire probate records and peculiar wills for the 18th and 19th centuries. www.eurekapartnership.com

POLL BOOKS AND ELECTORAL REGISTERS

Electoral registers were introduced in 1832 by the Representation of the People Act (also known as the 1832 Reform Act), and give the full names of everyone qualified to vote at a specific residence. At the time of its introduction, voting was restricted to men renting a property up to a particular value; by 1867 this was extended to all male householders.

Further reform acts in the twentieth century gradually introduced greater enfranchisement. Significantly, women were able to vote for the first time in 1918, but only those over the age of thirty who owned property. At the same time, property restrictions for men were lifted, so all men over the age of twenty could vote. Ten years later, equal voting rights were given to all men and women aged twenty-one and over. The voting age for men and women was lowered to eighteen in 1969.

Electoral registers can help confirm ancestors' full names, length of time at a particular address and family relationships.

OHC holds the original electoral registers for Oxfordshire and the City of Oxford. There are also copies on microfilm for Oxfordshire 1832–1938, City of Oxford 1823–1940 and Berkshire 1839–51. The Oxfordshire Registers of Electors 1832–2013, series EL1, is online via Heritage Search, or you can view them at the Centre, where there is also a parish index. Electoral registers are organised by street, and there are no surname indexes, so you need some idea of your ancestor's likely address. Read more in the OHC's Electoral Registers guide at www.oxfordshire.gov.uk/cms/content/running-county.

The OFHS has some electoral registers for 1865 and 1885 available to buy on microfiche (www.ofhs.org.uk/mfiche.html#er fiche).

Before the introduction of electoral registers, voters were listed in poll books. Again, voters had to meet certain property requirements, and only those who actually voted were listed. Information in poll books includes each voter's name, address, qualification for voting, location of the property that qualified them to vote and how they voted. Some included the occupation as well. Poll books date from 1696, and were discontinued in 1872 when the secret ballot was introduced.

The OHC holds some county poll books, and the BOD has poll books for the City of Oxford. You can also search Ancestry for UK poll books and electoral registers 1538–1893 at https://search.ancestry.co.uk/search/db.aspx?dbid=2410.

DIRECTORIES

Local telephone, street and trade directories provide a wealth of geographical and historical information about counties and towns, as well as listing traders, clergy, the gentry and, later on, ordinary householders. Produced annually, they capture people and places at a specific time and put them in an historical and social context. When consulting directories, bear in mind that they were published some time after the information was collected, so they could already have been out of date by the time they were printed. Nevertheless, they can be useful in tracing your ancestor's movements between the censuses and in the years before the census began.

Among the most useful are *Kelly's Directory* and *Pigot & Co.*, which include descriptions and historical information as well as detailed listings of a region's major towns and cities, businesses, tradesmen, landowners and charities.

The OHC has a large collection of county and town directories for Oxfordshire for 1783–1981, as well as some for Berkshire and Buckinghamshire. Towns covered include Abingdon, Banbury, Bicester, Burford, Faringdon, Henley-on-Thames, Wallingford, Wantage and Witney, as well as the city of Oxford. There are also telephone directories and Yellow Pages for Oxford, Banbury, Reading and the South Midlands covering the period 1914–2009. The website includes complete lists of both sets of directories, which are available at the Centre and can also be searched online via Heritage Search. You can also search directories online at www.historical directories.org.

NEWSPAPERS AND MAGAZINES

Local newspapers and other journals can provide all kinds of useful and fascinating information for family historians. Birth, marriage, death and funeral announcements can help clarify details such as dates, full name, names of relatives, occupation and place of residence, while stated preferences – such as flowers or donations to charity in funeral announcements – also tell you something about your ancestors.

Obituaries are another great source of information, usually giving birth and death dates and places, details of surviving family members and other biographical details that you might not find anywhere else – for example, membership of a local club or society, an unusual hobby or involvement in local politics.

Reviews of concerts and shows, reports of sports matches, school news and exam results, crime reports, court proceedings, inquests, business reports, local and national news items and advertisements can also reveal details of your ancestor's life and the place in which he or she lived.

The newspaper archive at OHC includes *The Oxford Times* (founded 1862) and its forerunners, *Jackson's Oxford Journal* (1753–1909) and *Oxford Journal* (1909–1928), as well as the *Oxford Mail* and many more local titles for both Oxfordshire and Berkshire. You can access these in a number of ways:

- Original copies of the majority of titles are on microfilm, arranged by date, and can be viewed in the OHC searchroom;
- The Oxfordshire People Index (which includes obituaries and other biographical items) and the Oxfordshire Business Index, covering 1800-2006, are online via Heritage Search;
- Eileen Davies' *The Synopsis and Index to Jackson's Oxford Journal, 1753–1790*, is in print, and a later version, extending to 1795 and including the Vale of White Horse, is on microfilm, both available in the searchroom;
- *News of a Country Town*, a compilation of extracts from *Jackson's Oxford Journal* relating to Abingdon 1753–1835, is available in the searchroom;
- Newspaper cuttings covering the 1970s are available online via Heritage Search;
- Newspaper cuttings 1980–2006 are arranged by subject for Oxfordshire, Oxford City and large Oxfordshire towns, and can be viewed in the searchroom;
- The Newsquest Oxfordshire newspaper archive, covering 2002–

2013, can be searched online at the OHC and includes all the local Newsquest titles – *Abingdon Herald*, *Banbury Cake*, *Bicester Advertiser*, *Didcot Herald*, *Oxford Mail*, *Oxford Star*, *The Oxford Times*, *Wallingford Herald*, *Wantage Herald* and *Witney Gazette*.

- Local and national newspapers are also available via Reference Online for Oxfordshire libraries members (see Chapter 1).

OHC also holds copies of county, parish and community magazines relating to Oxfordshire and Berkshire, national family history magazines and publications by local historical societies and businesses, all available in the searchroom. Publications produced by the Berkshire Record Society, Oxfordshire Record Society and Oxford Historical Society can be searched online via Heritage Search.

For more information about OHC's newspaper, magazine and directory holdings, visit https://www.oxfordshire.gov.uk/cms/ content/ newspapers-periodicals-and-directories.

MAPS

Maps can tell you a lot about the area in which your ancestor lived, including how it changed during your ancestor's lifetime and how much it has changed since. Buildings that no longer exist, such as factories, schools and houses, can be located on old maps. You can also see where farmland used to exist, where new roads have been built, and so on.

OHC has a large collection of printed maps, covering a period of more than 400 years. County maps date from 1579, the earliest being Christopher Saxton's *Atlas of England and Wales*. Oxfordshire is combined on one sheet with Berkshire and Buckinghamshire (ref. MPC 364). Roads are not shown, and the maps were produced to a very small scale, but you can see the location of villages and landmarks such as windmills and ancient parkland. Saxton paved the way for later county maps, which appeared throughout the seventeenth and early eighteenth centuries and gradually included more details including hundred boundaries, roads, rivers, fields, towns and villages.

Ordnance Survey maps first appeared in 1791 and have been regularly updated ever since, providing a detailed, large-scale record of the way our landscape has changed over more than 200 years.

Also useful are town plans, which were produced from the late sixteenth century, and thematic maps such as boundary maps, transport and tourist maps, and shopping centre maps. Other historic maps include tithe maps, enclosure maps, estate maps and district valuation maps.

OHC's holdings are listed in detail in the searchroom; some have been catalogued and can be identified through Heritage Search. For full details of OHC's map collection, visit www.oxfordshire.gov.uk/cms/content/maps-oxfordshire-history-centre.

The BOD has one of the largest collections of maps in the world, including atlases, journals, gazetteers, sheet maps and many rare items. The Map Room is located in the Weston Library and is open to anyone with a reader's card. Find out more at www.bodleian.ox.ac.uk/maps/about.

The OFHS has a small collection of maps available, including an Oxfordshire parish map (interactive version on the website; also available as a free download or A4 print), a City of Oxford parish map (free download or A3 print), an 1801 Oxfordshire Hundreds map and an Oxfordshire surname migration map. Visit www.ofhs.org.uk/ofhs.html for details.

PHOTOGRAPHS AND ORAL HISTORIES

OHC has a vast collection of historic images, prints and drawings of Oxfordshire and more than 5,000 oral history recordings, both of which you can search or browse via Picture Oxon (http://pictureoxon.com).

Some of the most significant image collections include:

- Henry Taunt collection of 14,000 images dating back to 1860;
- Percy Elford's photographs of Oxfordshire schools in the early twentieth century;

- Newsquest Oxfordshire Ltd archive 1930-2000, featuring images printed in *The Oxford Times* and the *Oxford Mail*;
- Oxford Journal Illustrated archive 1909-1928;
- Abingdon Museum and Banbury Museum collections, from 1880;
- Aerial photographs, including collections taken by Ordnance Survey, the RAF and the Department of the Environment.

Another good source of photographs is the Historic England Archive (http://archive.historicengland.org.uk), which has images from the 1850s to the present and is particularly good for domestic and industrial buildings. You need to register for a Heritage Passport before you can place orders. Registration is free.

OHC's oral history collection includes field recordings and extracts from Radio Oxford broadcasts made during the 1960s and 1970s. These capture people's memories of Oxfordshire life stretching back to the early twentieth century and include work, childhood, immigration and much more. For each topic, the website has a detailed list of what's available. You can listen to oral history recordings in the OHC searchroom, order copies online or listen to selected extracts featured on the website.

DIARIES AND PERSONAL PAPERS

Papers relating to individuals or families can be mini treasure troves, often containing items such as letters, diaries, photographs, financial papers, wills and other probate documents, family trees, family bibles, title deeds, registration papers and more. Collections held by the OHC can only be viewed in the searchroom, but some of the records are online at Heritage Search.

The BOD has a large collection of diaries and papers relating to prominent local and national figures, including those of physician Henry Acland, Ashmolean Museum founder Elias Ashmole, author William Beckford, Bishop Samuel Wilberforce (son of anti-slave trade campaigner William), composer Felix Mendelssohn and many others. Visit www.bodley.ox.ac.uk/dept/scwmss/wmss/online/ online.htm for a detailed list.

This vast collection of material, offering personal perspectives on local and national events, helps to capture aspects of Oxfordshire at particular moments in time and give a sense of what life was like for our ancestors.

FURTHER READING

Annal, David, *Easy Family History*, 2nd edition, Bloomsbury, 2013

Annal, David and Collins, Audrey, *Birth, Marriage and Death Records: A Guide for Family Historians*, Pen & Sword, 2012

Bates, Denise, *Historical Research Using British Newspapers*, Pen & Sword, 2016

Blanchard, Gill, *Writing Your Family History*, Pen & Sword, 2014

Fowler, Simon, *Family History: Digging Deeper*, The History Press, 2012

Foy, Karen, *Family History for Beginners*, The History Press, 2011

Grannum, Karen and Taylor, Nigel, *Wills and Probate Records*, The National Archives, 2009

Lisle, Nicola, *Tracing Your Family History Made Easy*, Which? Books, 2011

Oates, Jonathan, *Tracing Your Ancestors Through Local History Records*, Pen & Sword, 2016

Chapter 3

CHURCH OF ENGLAND AND NON-CONFORMITY

Henry VIII's accession to the throne in 1509 marked the beginning of major religious reform in England and Wales, with Protestantism replacing Roman Catholicism as the established Church. In 1534, Henry VIII severed ties with the Church of Rome and became head of the Church of England by the Act of Supremacy. The twelfth-century Osney Abbey in West Oxford briefly became the cathedral of the new diocese of Oxford before Henry handed that honour to Christ Church in 1545. Osney and other local abbeys were

Christ Church College and Cathedral, which has been the cathedral for the Diocese of Oxford since 1545. © Nicola Lisle

demolished during the Dissolution of the Monasteries. These sweeping reforms heralded the beginning of an organized, official system of record-keeping.

PARISH REGISTERS AND BISHOPS' TRANSCRIPTS

Parish registers were introduced in 1538 by Thomas Cromwell, Henry VIII's Vicar-General, who ordered Anglican clergymen to start keeping weekly registers of all baptisms, marriages and burials in their parish. At the time, the parish was the main unit of civic and ecclesiastical administration in England and Wales, resulting in a vast body of records that provide crucial links to our ancestors' lives going back to the early sixteenth century. Once you have discovered as much as you can from the BMD indexes and census returns, the parish records should enable you to take your family tree back a few more generations.

Early record-keeping was haphazard. Not all parishes complied with Cromwell's order, and those that did often used loose sheets of poor-quality paper that were subsequently lost or illegible. Few records from before 1600 have survived.

From 1598, parish registers had to be written into parchment books and duplicates submitted annually to the diocesan bishop. The latter resulted in another useful set of records known as the Bishops' Transcripts. Sometimes the Bishops' Transcripts contain details not found in the parish registers, and in some cases have survived where parish registers have not, so it is worth checking both sets of records.

Lord Hardwicke's Marriage Act came into force in 1754 to prevent illicit marriages – its full name was 'An Act for the Better Preventing of Clandestine Marriage' – and required all marriages, except those of Quakers and Jews, to be conducted in an Anglican church after the calling of banns, with the marriages and banns to be recorded in separate, pre-printed registers.

Marriage licences, a useful alternative to banns if the couple wanted to avoid publicity or wanted a quick wedding, were issued by the ecclesiastical courts on payment of a bond that was forfeit if the marriage either did not take place or was later found to be unlawful.

Rose's Act of 1812 came into force on 1 January 1813 and introduced standardised printed registers for baptisms and burials.

What the parish registers will tell you

Baptisms

- Before 1812: child's name, date of baptism, father's occupation, sometimes parents' names, date of birth.
- After 1812: As above, plus place of baptism, parents' names (mother only if child was illegitimate), place of residence, sometimes date of birth.

Marriages

- Before 1754: date of marriage, names of bride and groom, other information variable (according to parish).
- After 1754: As above, plus place of marriage, groom's home parish, bride's maiden name and home parish, whether married by licence or banns, status (i.e. spinster, bachelor, widow, widower), signatures of bride and groom, names and signatures of two witnesses, name of officiating clergyman.
- Marriage banns: varies, but usually includes brides' and grooms' addresses, ages, status, parents' names if under 21.
- Marriage licences: again varies, but usually brides' and grooms' ages, occupations, status, parents' details.

Note that marriage banns and licences are not proof that a marriage actually took place, so always check the marriage registers as well.

Burials

- Before 1812: Name of deceased, date of burial, sometimes age, occupation, marital status, parents' names in the case of infant deaths.

- After 1812: As above, plus age, date of death, address at time of death, cause of death, sometimes occupation.

Where to find parish registers

The OHC holds most of the surviving pre-1900 parish registers and bishops' transcripts for more than 300 parishes within the Archdeaconry of Oxfordshire, which equates roughly to the pre-1974 county boundaries. Records for the former North Berkshire parishes (the Vale of White Horse) are held by the BRO. The OHC's registers are not available to view online, but you can search the parish catalogues using Heritage Search. Enter 'PAR' followed by the parish you are interested in. If you can't find what you are looking for you will need to view the printed catalogue in the searchroom.

The OFHS has produced transcripts of parish registers and bishops' transcripts for Oxfordshire and the former North Berkshire parishes, and these are available to buy on CD. Details of parishes and the dates are covered are available on the society's book sales page: www.ofhs.org.uk/MH2016-sales-pages.pdf.

Other useful sources include:

- The SoG (www.sog.org.uk) has the UK's largest collection of parish register copies and transcripts for England and Wales. It also holds the original Boyd's Marriage Index, which has more than 7 million names compiled from local parish registers, bishops' transcripts and marriage licences from 1538–1840 and can be searched via Findmypast. Details include full names of the bride and groom, year of marriage, county and parish in which the marriage took place and source of the record.
- The International Genealogical Index (IGI) was compiled from original parish registers, bishops' transcripts and non-parochial registers by the CJCLDS and has now been incorporated into their Family Search website: www.familysearch.org/search/collection/igi.
- The National Burial Index was compiled by the FFHS to

complement the IGI, and contains over 18 million names drawn from parish, non-conformist, Roman Catholic, Quaker and cemetery registers for the period 1538–2008. It is available to buy from the FFHS (www.ffhs.org.uk/burials/nbi-v3.php) or you can search the index via Findmypast. Details include full name of the deceased, date of burial, age if given, place where burial was recorded and the name of the recording society or individual.

- The PA holds surviving protestation returns from 1641–42, when all men over the age of eighteen were required to swear an oath of allegiance to the Crown, Parliament and the Protestant religion. Lists of names were compiled by each parish and submitted to Parliament. Returns have been digitised and can be searched on the PA's online catalogue, Portcullis (www.portcullis.parliament.uk). The main series of Oxfordshire protestation returns is HL/PO/JO/10/1/102, and you can search for individual parishes within that series. You may also find the following useful: BOOK/4617 (Index to Oxfordshire protestation oath returns 1641-42); BOOK/4673 (Oxfordshire protestation returns 1641/42 transcribed and edited); BOOK/2857 (Oxfordshire and North Berkshire Protestation Returns and Tax Assessments 1641–42).

NON-CONFORMISTS AND OTHER FAITHS

In many parts of Oxfordshire, people resisted Henry VIII's reforms and clung to their Roman Catholic beliefs. At Stonor Park, near Henley-on-Thames, the Stonor family provided refuge for Jesuit priest and missionary Edmund Campion, who set up a secret printing press there and produced his pro-Catholic treatise *Decem Rationes*, which he distributed around Oxford. Campion was imprisoned in the Tower of London in July 1581 and repeatedly tortured before being tried and found guilty of sedition. He was hung, drawn and quartered at Tyburn on 1 December 1581. In 1970, he was canonised by Pope Paul VI as one of the Forty Martyrs of England and Wales.

A more notorious local agitator was Robert Catesby, who lived for a while at nearby Chastleton House, and was one of Guy Fawkes' co-conspirators in the Gunpowder Plot. Much of their plotting was carried out in the Catherine Wheel inn, which stood in Broad Street on part of the current Balliol College site.

During the seventeenth century, dissident groups began to break away from the Anglican Church to form their own congregations. Among the earliest were the Baptists, established in 1611, and the Society of Friends – more commonly known as the Quakers – which was founded by George Fox in 1647. Both became popular quickly, and there were soon several Baptist churches and Friends' Meeting Houses scattered throughout Oxfordshire.

Oxford University gave birth to Methodism in 1729 when brothers John and Charles Wesley were instrumental in forming the 'Holy Club', whose members engaged in regular study, prayer, fasting and meditation. They were also committed to social work, and became regular visitors to Oxford Prison. A plaque in New Inn Hall Street, in the centre of Oxford, marks the site of the city's first Methodist meeting house, where John Wesley preached on several occasions. Close by is the Wesley Memorial Methodist Church.

The University was also the cradle for the Oxford Movement, which began in the 1830s as a reaction against what its members perceived as the increasing secularisation of the Church of England. Between 1833 and 1841 they produced *Tracts for the Times*, a collection of ninety theological books and essays urging a return to the greater spirituality of the Catholic church. The collection was written by some of the movement's leading advocates, including John Henry Newman (later Cardinal Newman, following his conversion to Roman Catholicism); clergyman Edward Pusey, co-founder of Keble College; and clergyman and poet John Keble, after whom Keble College was named.

Non-conformist records

Even after breaking away from the Anglican church, many non-

John Wesley plaque in New Inn Hall Street, Oxford. © Nicola Lisle

conformists continued to appear in the parish registers because the parish church was the only place where they could be married or buried. Following the introduction of civil registration in 1837, many non-conformist registers were sent to the General Register Office under the Non-Parochial Registers Act and are now held by TNA. Records for Oxfordshire can be found in RG4 (Registers of Births, Marriages and Deaths surrendered to the Non-Parochial Registers Commissions of 1837 and 1857) and RG6 (Society of Friends' Registers, Notes and Certificates of Births, Marriages and Deaths). The TNA's guide to non-conformist records has useful information and links: www.nationalarchives.gov.uk/help-with-your-research/research-guides/nonconformists.

The EP has produced sixteen volumes of transcripts relating to Methodist circuits and Congregational and Baptist churches in Abingdon, Witney, Thame, Chipping Norton, Oxford, Henley-on-Thames, Hook Norton, Wantage and Wallingford. www.eurekapartnership.com

The SoG also holds records relating to Roman Catholics, Jews and the non-conformist religions, including lists of ministers and copies of some pre-1837 non-conformist registers.

Details of local records and other sources for different non-Anglican religions are given below.

Baptists

OHC has registers of baptisms, marriages and burials from the nineteenth century onwards for the Baptist churches at Hook Norton, Thame, Bloxham, Chipping Norton, Banbury, Eynsham and South Oxford. These registers have been transcribed and are on open shelves in the searchroom. The collection also includes administrative records including minutes, accounts, membership registers and Sunday School records.

The Angus Library and Archive (http://theangus.rpc.ox.ac.uk) at Regent's Park College, Oxford, is the world's leading collection of Baptist history and incorporates the collections of the Baptist Union of Great Britain, Baptist Historical Society, Baptist Missionary Society and *The Baptist Times*. Holdings include church records, church histories, manuscript letters, books, pamphlets, journals and the papers of leading Baptist families. Visits to the library are by appointment only.

The Baptist History Society website has tips on researching Baptist family history (http://baptisthistory.org.uk/discover/family-history) and provides useful links.

Quakers

Quakers have always been particularly efficient at keeping records, which is good news for family historians. Birth, marriage and death records are at the TNA (see above), but OHC has a large collection of records from the seventeenth century onwards, including records of meetings, minute books, administrative and financial papers relating to Quaker meeting houses, correspondence, photographs and many more miscellaneous papers. The main series are NQ1 (Banbury Monthly Meeting), NQ2 (Vale Monthly Meeting) and NQ3 (Witney Monthly Meeting). Use Heritage Search to see the full holdings, which can be viewed in the OHC searchroom. Records for Quaker meetings in former Berkshire towns are held at the BRO.

The Friends Meeting House in London (www.quaker.org.uk/library) is useful if you want to find out more about the history of the Quakers, and there is a downloadable PDF on Genealogy in the collection of subject guides.

Methodists

Methodist chapels are grouped into circuits, usually served by a team of ministers but occasionally only having one minister. OHC holds records for the circuits of Chipping Norton and Stow (NM1), Witney and Faringdon (NM2), Thame and Watlington (NM3), Banbury (NM4), Oxford (NM5), and Wantage and Abingdon (NM6), dating from the early nineteenth century. Records include chapel and circuit birth and marriage registers, which have been transcribed and are available on open shelves. The Oxford circuit collection also includes records for The John Wesley Society.

The CBS holds records for Bicester, as this comes under the Buckingham, Brackley and Bicester circuit, and also for Aylesbury Vale Circuit, which includes some chapels previously in the Thame and Watlington circuit.

The Oxfordshire circuits are part of the Oxfordshire and Leicestershire District, so any records not at the OHC will be held at the Leicestershire Record Office (www.leicestershire.gov.uk/registrars/trace-your-family-tree/researching-your-family-history).

OBUSC holds the Wesley Historical Society Library (www.brookes.ac.uk/hpc/research/oxford-centre-for-methodism-and-church-history/special-collections), which includes collections of historic circuit plans, unofficial national surveys of Methodist churches, images of Wesleyan ministers and other Methodists, Wesleyan conference memorabilia and archives of the Wesley Historical Society.

For more on the history of Methodism, the Methodist Archives and Research Centre (MARC) at the University of Manchester Library (www.library.manchester.ac.uk/search-resources/guide-to-special-collections/methodist) is worth exploring. The Centre holds the world's largest collection of letters, notebooks and other papers relating to John and Charles Wesley, as well as the personal papers of other prominent Methodists, ministers and lay-ministers, and the administrative collections deposited by Methodist churches. There is a downloadable guide to the resources.

Congregationalists and United Reform Church

The Congregational Church was formed during the mid-seventeenth century and was run by deacons and elders. They were also known in the early years as Independents and later as Unitarians. In 1972, the Congregational Church merged with the Presbyterians to form the United Reformed Church.

OHC holds records for Independent, Congregational and United Reformed Churches in Summertown, Banbury, Frilford, Thame, Bicester, Wheatley, Witney, Deddington, Kingston Blount and Oxford (St Columba's, Temple Cowley and George Street) in series NC1–NC9. Collections include baptism, marriage and burial registers and church administration records.

The Congregational Collections at Dr Williams's Library in London (www.dwl.ac.uk) has archives containing local history and records of churches, training and work of ministers, diaries, correspondence, institutional records and more than 50,000 books, pamphlets and periodicals covering the history of the Congregational Church and other dissenting religions.

Roman Catholics

After the Act of Supremacy, Roman Catholics suffered persecution for over 200 years, during which they were subject to harsh laws and punishments. Persecution ceased in the eighteenth century, but it wasn't until the Catholic Emancipation Act of 1829 that restrictions were lifted on Catholics being able to enter the professions, hold official offices or inherit land. This generated a great many records relating to Catholics' activities, fines and punishments.

The OHC holds some records for specific churches, including Eynsham Catholic and Apostolic Church, St Thomas More Catholic Church in Kidlington and St Aloysius Catholic Church in Oxford,

Oxford Oratory Church of St Aloysius Gonzaga, the Catholic parish church for Oxford, completed 1875. © Nicola Lisle

and these mainly consist of marriage and service attendance registers. The Diocesan collection includes lists of ex-communicants and recusants, papist returns, churchwardens' presentments, dissenting meeting house returns and some family papers. There are also some relevant records in the Quarter Sessions catalogues, which you can locate using Heritage Search.

The PA (www.parliament.uk/archives) holds papist returns for the years 1680, 1706, 1767 and 1781, and the website includes information and tips on searching.

TNA also has records relating to Catholics and recusancy; see their guide www.nationalarchives.gov.uk/help-with-your-research /research-guides/catholics.

The Catholic Family History Society (www.catholicfhs.online) has published a range of useful resources, which are available for purchase through the website. This includes the Margaret Higgins Database, which was released in October 2017 and holds records of around 275,000 Catholics living in England between 1607 and 1840. Compiled by Australian monk Brother Rory Higgins, the details were drawn from papist returns from the 18th century as well as a variety of other sources.

Jews

For just over 200 years, from around 1075 to 1290, there was a significant Jewish settlement in Oxford, stretching from Carfax, in the centre of the city, to the southern end of St Aldates, which was then known as Great Jewry Street and was a bustling market area. The current Town Hall stands on the site of a group of five medieval Jewish houses, while the Rose Garden in High Street, just outside the Botanic Gardens, conceals the medieval Jewish cemetery. A memorial stone was erected in November 2016 to mark the former burial site. All Jews were expelled from England by King Edward I in 1290, and it was not until the seventeenth century that Jews began to return to Oxford and its surrounds. Visit www.oxfordjewishheritage.co.uk to find out more about the history of the Jewish community in Oxford.

The modern Oxford Jewish Congregation (www.oxford-synagogue.org.uk) was founded in 1842, with the consecration of Oxford's first synagogue, in Richmond Road, taking place in January 1893. This was replaced with a new synagogue on the same site in April 1974. The OHC holds administrative and financial records for the Oxford Jewish Congregation (series O26) from 1930, including reports, minutes and other records relating to Jewish charitable and youth organisations, social and friendship clubs, the planning and building of the Oxford Synagogue and Jewish Centre, and more. The BOD also holds some records relating to the Jewish community dating back to 1881 (MS Top. Oxon d.486-488).

For details of births, marriages and deaths of Jews in the Oxford area, contact the Oxford Register Office (www.oxfordshire.gov.uk/cms/content/registration-offices).

The current Oxford Jewish cemetery is within Wolvercote Cemetery in North Oxford (sections K1-K5 and M3) and was consecrated in 1894. You can download a PDF of burials from the Oxford Jewish Heritage website at www.oxfordjewishheritage.co.uk /images/stories/Wolvercote/Wolvercotejoct2017. Burials are listed by section, and for each burial give the grave number, full name, age at death and date of burial.

Other useful resources include the TNA's guide www.national archives.gov.uk/help-with-your-research-guides/jews-and-jewish-communities-18th-20th-centuries and JewishGen (www.jewish gen.org), which has millions of searchable records as well as lots of helpful advice and links to other relevant databases, and also offers a Jewish genealogy course.

GRAVES AND MONUMENTAL INSCRIPTIONS

Before the nineteenth century, burials are likely to have taken place in the deceased's home parish, including those of dissenters. It was not until the passing of various Burial Acts between the 1850s and 1880s that local authorities began opening cemeteries for non-conformists and other faiths.

Visiting the final resting places of your ancestors can provide an emotional link that no document ever can, and their headstones often carry useful biographical details as well as revealing other clues about their lives. The information given on headstones obviously varies greatly, but in addition to the deceased's full name, date (or year) of death and age at death, you will almost certainly discover names of other family members and their relationship to the deceased. It is not unusual to find several members of one family listed on a gravestone, which can enable you to add details to your family tree or give you clues for further research.

Other details you might come across include:

- Date and place of birth
- Cause of death

Gravestone inscriptions sometimes list several family members, like this gravestone for the Poulton family in Holywell Cemetery, Oxford. © Nicola Lisle

- Occupation and/or military service
- Official titles and/or qualifications
- Quotes from the Bible or other texts, symbols and decorations, all of which can indicate religious denomination, favourite religious or literary works, hobbies or occupation.

The Victorians were particularly keen on elaborate carvings on gravestones, usually in the form of religious symbols or depictions of tools indicating a person's trade, such as agricultural implements. In Oxfordshire's 'wool' towns of Witney, Chipping Norton and Burford, for example, you will often find wool bales or wool manufacturers' tools carved onto gravestones (see Chapter 5).

Gravestones can also give you clues about your ancestor's wealth and social status. A family vault, for example, indicates wealth and prominence in the local community; you will also find that the graves of wealthier families are positioned in prominent positions near the church or inside the church.

A problem with gravestone inscriptions, of course, is that many have become worn and are either difficult to decipher or completely illegible. In addition, gravestones may have been moved or destroyed. Fortunately, many monumental inscriptions (MIs) have been transcribed and preserved, and are an invaluable resource for family historians. The OHC has MIs within the parish collections (PAR), as well as volumes of MIs from the twentieth century for various churches and churchyards in Oxfordshire (P188). In addition, the OFHS has produced transcriptions of MIs for a large number of Oxfordshire churchyards and cemeteries, and these are available to purchase on CD or microfiche.

Other useful resources include the SoG, which has one of the UK's largest collections of MI transcriptions (www.sog.org.uk/sogat/access), and the Gravestone Photographic Resource (www.gravestonephotos.com), an ongoing project that records monuments from all over the world and currently has details and images for nearly thirty Oxfordshire churchyards, cemeteries and war memorials.

For more on war graves and memorials, see Chapter 8.

PLACES TO VISIT

Stonor Park

The history of this medieval country house, home to the Stonor family for 850 years, has been shaped by the persecution of Catholics following the accession of Henry VIII. There is a permanent exhibition of the life and death of Jesuit martyr Edmund Campion,

Find out about the history of Dorchester Abbey at the local museum © Nicola Lisle

and you can see the rooms where he established his secret press and printed *Decem Rationes.* www.stonor.com/st-edmond-campion

Dorchester Abbey Museum

The story of Dorchester Abbey and Dorchester village is told through a range of artefacts and carvings, displayed in the Abbey's Cloister Gallery and the sixteenth-century school room in the adjoining Abbey Guest House. www.dorchester-abbey.org.uk/ museum.htm

FURTHER READING

Parish Records

Gibson, J.S.W., *Bishops' Transcripts and Marriage Licences, Bonds and Allegations*, Federation of Family History Societies, 1991

Gibson, Jeremy and Dell, Alan, The Protestation Returns, 1641–42, and Other Contemporary Listings, FFHS, 1995

Raymond, Stuart A., *Parish Registers, A History and Guide*, The Family History Partnership, 2009

Raymond, Stuart A., *Tracing Your Ancestors' Parish Records*, Pen & Sword, 2015
Raymond, Stuart, A., *Tracing Your Church of England Ancestors*, Pen & Sword, 2017
Steel, D.J., *National Index of Parish Registers, Vol.1: Sources of births, marriages and deaths before 1837*, Society of Genealogists, 1968

Non-conformists

Breed, Geoffrey R., *My Ancestors were Baptists*, Society of Genealogists, 2007
Clifford, David J.H., *My Ancestors were Congregationalists in England and Wales*, Society of Genealogists, 1997
Gandy, Michael, *Tracing Non-Conformist Ancestors*, TNA, 2001
Leary, W. and Gandy, M., *My Ancestors were Methodists*, Society of Genealogists, 1982
Milligan, E.H. and Thomas, M.J., *My Ancestors were Quakers*, Society of Genealogists, 2005
Ratcliffe, Richard, *Basic Facts about Methodist Records for Family Historians*, Federation of Family History Societies, 2005
Raymond, Stuart A., *Birth and Baptism Records for Family Historians*, Family History Partnership, 2010
Raymond, Stuart A., *Tracing Your Non-Conformist Ancestors*, Pen & Sword, 2017
Ruston, Alan *My Ancestors were English Presbyterians/Unitarians*, Society of Genealogists, 2001

Roman Catholics

Gandy, Michael, *Tracing Your Catholic Ancestors*, TNA, 2001

Jews

Lewis, David M., *The Jews of Oxford*, Oxford Jewish Congregation, 1992
Wenzerul, Rosemary, *Tracing Your Jewish Ancestors*, Pen & Sword, 2008

Chapter 4

HEALTHCARE, POVERTY AND CRIME

Before the introduction of the Welfare State and the National Health Service in the mid-twentieth century, responsibility for looking after the aged, the infirm and the poor lay with the local authorities. From the sixteenth century, various laws existed to ensure that every parish provided practical, financial or medical support to locals who were destitute or sick. Over the centuries this generated all kinds of records that can be of great value to family historians.

LOCAL HOSPITALS AND HEALTHCARE

There was no universal system of healthcare in the UK until the founding of the National Health Service in 1948. Hospitals, infirmaries and asylums were established by local parishes and councils, Poor Law unions, charities and wealthy benefactors, and many were overseen by voluntary governing bodies. Subscription hospitals became popular among the wealthy during the eighteenth century, although they did admit a limited number of poor people for treatment if they were given a special recommendation. Some of the great pioneering hospitals also began to emerge in UK cities during the eighteenth century, while the nineteenth century saw the spread of specialist hospitals, sanatoriums and nursing and convalescent homes.

Oxford's first hospital, the Radcliffe Infirmary, opened in 1770 as a charitable hospital for the poor, funded by money from

Dr John Radcliffe's estate and built on land donated by Thomas Rowney, the Conservative MP for Oxford from 1722–59. The hospital expanded rapidly, adding extra wards during its first two years, and gradually adding other departments and facilities. In 1941 the Radcliffe created medical history by administering the first dose of penicillin to a patient (an event now marked with a blue plaque), and by opening the UK's first accident department. The hospital closed in 2007, with all departments being transferred to the John Radcliffe Hospital, which opened in Headington in 1972, initially as a maternity hospital. It is now Oxford's principal hospital, and the main teaching hospital for Oxford University and Oxford Brookes University (see Chapter 7).

Like the rest of the UK, Oxfordshire suffered repeated epidemics of cholera, smallpox and other deadly diseases. Several infectious diseases and isolation hospitals opened in the county during the nineteenth century, including in Abingdon, Banbury, Chipping Norton, Henley, Wallingford and Witney. A number of asylums also emerged during the nineteenth century, notably the Warneford Hospital (originally the Radcliffe Asylum) in 1826 and Littlemore Hospital in 1846. Batt's Madhouse in Witney was founded by Edward Batt in 1823 to care for those suffering from 'diseases of the mind', and continued to be run by members of the Batt family until its closure in 1857.

During the twentieth century, important specialist and research hospitals were established in Oxford, including the Churchill Hospital (1942) and the Wingfield-Morris Orthopaedic Hospital, now the Nuffield Orthopaedic Centre (1933). The latter was funded by car manufacturer William Morris, later Lord Nuffield (see chapter 6).

Dr John Radcliffe: Oxford's Leading Physician

Yorkshire-born medical pioneer John Radcliffe became one of the leading physicians of his day in Oxford and London. After being educated at Wakefield Grammar School, he came up to University College, Oxford, in 1665, becoming a Fellow of Lincoln College at the age of twenty-one. He set up a medical practice in Oxford in 1675, and was soon upsetting colleagues and local apothecaries with his bluntness and his unconventional methods.

When a smallpox epidemic swept through the city in the late seventeenth century, Radcliffe confounded his critics by advocating better personal hygiene, common sense and fresh air instead of the established treatments, and most of his patients recovered.

He became a favourite with the nobility after he successfully treated Sir Thomas Spencer, Lord of the Manor at Yarnton, for a long-standing illness. In 1684 he moved to London and quickly became the capital's most sought-after physician, notably treating William III for smallpox after two other physicians had failed.

He died in 1714, aged sixty-five, and was buried at the University Church, Oxford. His name lives on in the city in Radcliffe Square, the Radcliffe Camera, the Radcliffe Observatory, the former Radcliffe Infirmary and the John Radcliffe Hospital.

Local archives

The Oxfordshire Health Archives (www.oxfordshirehealtharchives.nhs.uk) is the main repository for records relating to Oxfordshire hospitals, NHS administrative bodies, League of Friends and nurses' training. The collection is based at the OHC and can be viewed in the OHC searchroom. You can also locate records using OHC's Heritage Search and TNA Discovery. Note that patient records are closed for 100 years from the date of death, and administrative records for thirty years.

The OHA's website has lots of useful information and tips on searching. A good starting point is the comprehensive list of private and NHS hospitals, which gives for each a brief history, a list of the records available and other possible sources of information. Records vary greatly from one hospital to another and may include any of the following:

- Admission, discharge and death registers
- Registers of operations
- Nursing staff records
- Nurse training records
- Patient records and case notes
- Matrons' report books
- Visitors' books
- Newsletters
- Scrap books
- Financial and administrative papers, e.g. minutes, annual reports, accounts and building plans
- Photographs

The survival of early patient and staff records is somewhat patchy. Only six hospitals have patient records pre-dating 1920: Radcliffe Infirmary, Oxford Eye Hospital, Littlemore Asylum (later Littlemore Hospital), Warneford Hospital, Brackley Cottage Hospital and Horton General Hospital in Banbury. Burial records for deceased patients exist only for Radcliffe Infirmary and Littlemore Hospital. Individual staff records exist only for Radcliffe Infirmary, Littlemore Hospital and Warneford Hospital, although details of appointment and leaving dates for senior staff only often appear in reports and minute books, along with disciplinary offences and dismissals.

For patient and staff records, it will save a lot of time if you know which hospital your ancestor was in and approximate dates. Census records, civil and parish registers, probate records, obituaries, court records, charity records, war records, personal papers and oral history recordings are all possible sources for this information.

The OHC holds collections of records relating to some

Oxfordshire hospitals and health organisations. There are few patient or staffing records, but individuals may be named in other documents, particularly minutes and correspondence. The collections most likely to be of some use are listed below, together with series reference numbers and main contents.

H1 Littlemore Asylum 1841–1948.
Minute books, reports, correspondence, financial records, plans and specifications.

H2 Records of the Medical Officer of Health for Oxfordshire 1901–1974.
Notification of births, infectious diseases, stillbirths and infant deaths; nurses' records, midwives' records and health visitors' records.

H3 South Oxfordshire (Medical Officer of Health) Joint Committee 1910–1974.
Foundation records, minute books, correspondence, financial records.

H4 Oxford Regional Hospital Board 1947–1974.
Reports, handbooks, minutes, nursing records, nurse training committee reports, site plans.

H5 Oxford Regional Health Authority 1974–1994
Minutes, reports, workshop papers and correspondence relating to the Oxford Eye Hospital and various medical departments.

H8 Chipping Norton and Witney Urban and Rural Districts Joint Isolation Hospital 1902–1931.
Records of an isolation hospital set up at Shipton-under-Wychwood in 1902 to treat smallpox.
Inventories, correspondence, minute books, financial records, general ledgers.

H9 Buckinghamshire, Oxfordshire and Reading Joint Board for the Mentally Defective 1926-1948.
Administrative papers, correspondence, minutes.

National resources

TNA's series MH contains records for the Ministry of Health (1919–68) and its successors the Department of Health and Social Security (1968–88) and the Department of Health (from 1988), as well as local government boards and other related organisations, some dating back to 1798. These cover both health and Poor Law matters and include minute books, correspondence, personal papers and official reports. See also TNA's research guides to hospitals, mental health and asylums, patients, nurses and doctors.

The Wellcome Library's Archives and Manuscripts Collection has a vast collection of records and books relating to hospitals, healthcare professionals, mental health, maternity care, military medical care and more. Browse their research guides at https://wellcomelibrary.org/collections/archive-guides.

If you have nursing ancestors, the Royal College of Nursing Library and Heritage Centre (www.rcn.org.uk/library/services/family-history) has records relating to nurses and nursing history. The website includes a series of downloadable research guides, which include lots of useful information and tips.

The Royal College of Surgeons of England Archives (www.rcseng.ac.uk/museums-and-archives/archives) has deposited collections relating to surgeons and the surgical profession including personal papers, case notes, hospital records, correspondence, diaries, lecture notes, minute books of clubs and societies and photographs. Similarly, the Royal College of Physicians' archive (www.rcplondon.ac.uk/archive-and-historical-library-collections) contains manuscripts and personal papers as well as rare books and papers relating to medical research.

From the early sixteenth century, all physicians and surgeons in England and Wales were required to have licences before they could practise medicine. Licences were issued by local bishops or the Archbishop of Canterbury and recorded in bishops' and archbishops' registers. The Lambeth Palace Library has a downloadable index of medical licences issued from 1535–1775 (www.lambethpalacelibrary.org/files/Medical-Licences.pdf), which is searchable by surname or county. Details include name, parish and date licence was issued. Some give additional details, such as 'literate', 'gent' or 'yeoman'.

The library and archives of The Worshipful Society of Apothecaries of London holds records relating to apothecaries (www.apothecaries.org/charity/history/enquiries-access) including examination records, apprenticeship bindings, membership records, candidates' entry books and lists of licentiates. The website has a downloadable family history guide.

LOOKING AFTER THE POOR

Before 1834, care for the destitute was in the hands of the overseers of the poor, who were responsible for collecting poor rates from local parishioners, redistributing the money to those in need and keeping records of these transactions. Various local Acts from the late seventeenth century saw the building of the earliest workhouses, many of which had schools attached. In 1782, Gilbert's Act enabled groups of parishes to jointly fund local workhouses and workhouse schools, thereby saving money.

The Poor Law Amendment Act of 1834 was a significant milestone in the way the nation cared for the poor. A new Poor Law Commission was set up to oversee the establishment of Poor Law Unions, each of which consisted of a group of thirty to forty parishes and covered a ten-mile radius. Each Poor Law Union was headed by a Board of Guardians, which was responsible for assessing applications for poor relief, liaising with the parish churchwardens and overseers of the poor, managing the distribution of relief to the poor and ensuring that a workhouse was set up and maintained. Outdoor relief – whereby those suffering temporary hardship could remain in their own homes – was gradually phased out, and all able-bodied poor were sent to the workhouse.

In 1836 the Poor Law Commission became the Poor Law Board, changing again in 1871 to the Local Government Board. Poor laws continued to evolve throughout the nineteenth century, with further Poor Law Unions being set up and each Board of Guardians taking on increasing responsibilities such as sanitation, vaccinations and, from 1897, care of infants under the Infant Life Protection Act. From 1911, children's homes were provided for pauper children aged three to sixteen.

In 1930 county and borough councils took over the responsibilities of the Boards of Guardians under the direction of the newly-formed Ministry of Health. The Poor Law remained in force until the establishment of the Welfare State. Workhouses either became hospitals or were closed down.

Poor law records

Poor law records can reveal a lot about your ancestors, including their home parish(es), trade, apprenticeships, whether they paid or received poor relief and whether they held parish offices such as clergyman or churchwarden. Records date from the sixteenth century, and include overseers account books, churchwardens' accounts, parish rates books and vestry minutes.

Following the Settlement Act of 1662, settlement certificates were issued by an individual's home parish to certify that they would pay for that person's welfare if they became ill or destitute. Initially, certificates were only issued to migrant workers, but after 1697 they were issued to anyone deemed likely to fall on hard times. The certificates included the holder's name, home parish and signatures of the overseers of the poor, churchwardens and two witnesses.

If someone became destitute while away from their home parish, the local magistrate would undertake a settlement examination and often issued a Removal Order to return them to that parish. Settlement examination documents contained detailed biographical information, but sadly few have survived.

Local overseers often arranged apprenticeships for children of paupers, which in Oxfordshire usually meant they became agricultural labourers or went into domestic service. An apprenticeship indenture legally bound a child to the master of a specific trade or occupation, and was paid for by the overseers of the poor or by charitable bequests. The indenture included the child's name; the master's name, address and occupation; apprenticeship dates; whether the apprenticeship was completed; and sometimes the names and address of the child's parents.

Unmarried mothers with no financial support became the responsibility of the parish. The Bastardy Act of 1575/76 empowered local officials to establish the father's identity and make him pay maintenance for the child. Bastardy examinations, bonds and affiliation orders can be very helpful in clarifying ancestors' parentage as they include the father's name, place of birth, address, occupation, employees and parental details, as well as the mother's name and address.

Workhouse records include admission and discharge details, birth and death dates, rate books, medical officers' reports, vaccination lists, correspondence about inmates and staff records. Few have survived from before 1834. Workhouse inmates were included in the census returns, so it can be useful to cross-reference the two (see Chapter 2 for more about census returns).

The new Poor Law Unions from 1834 created a range of records, most notably the Board of Guardians minute books, which include details of poor law payouts, medical officers' reports, childcare details, and administrative and financial records of institutions.

Local records

OHC has a near-complete set of Board of Guardians minute books, as well as assessment committee papers, rate books, collection and deposit books, some workhouse records and other poor law papers. The catalogue for the Poor Law Union series (PLU1-PLU8) is online and in the searchroom. Earlier poor law records are held in some of the parish and borough collections (PAR10-PAR98 and BOR1-BOR4). The survival of records varies greatly from one borough or parish to another, but they may include overseers' and churchwardens' accounts, vestry minutes, rate books, poor rate appeal papers, collection and deposit books, valuation lists, collectors' monthly statements, apprenticeship indentures and other related papers.

Quarter Sessions records include bastardy papers, settlement papers and appeals. These are online from 1831 (QS1831-QS1856); earlier Quarter Sessions papers, from 1687, are only available in the OHC searchroom.

Other records only available in the searchroom include the Board of Guardians minute books for the Oxford Corporation for 1918-1930 (OCA/W.4.19-23), the Board of Guardians Annual Reports for the Oxford Incorporation 1873-1830 (hard copy) and the *Banbury Guardian or Monthly Poor Law register* for 1838–1843 (microfilm).

Local newspapers often reported on the building of new workhouses and other workhouse-related news, Board of Guardians meetings and staff appointments, and also carried advertisements for workhouse staff. Obituaries of inmates and staff were also included. Use Heritage Search to find relevant items.

The OFHS has produced an Oxford City Poor Law Index for 1853–1929 and Faringdon Bastardy Orders for 1868–1904, both available on microfiche, and Oxford City Guardians of the Poor reports for 1875–1915 on CD. Books include three volumes of bastardy trials for Oxford City covering 1832–1880, *Oxfordshire Bastardy Cases 1844–1909*, *Banbury Workhouse Records 1835–1843* and five volumes on Oxfordshire workhouse children 1850–1900.

For parishes previously in Berkshire, see the BFHS's Berkshire Overseers Project, which has brought together details from all surviving Poor Law documents for Berkshire from 1601-1834 and includes the Poor Law Unions of Abingdon, Faringdon, Wallingford and Wantage. Find out more about the project at www.berksfhs.org.uk/cms/Projects-general/berkshire-overseers-project.html. You can also purchase the CD from the society at www.berksfhs. org.uk/shop.

National resources

TNA's collections include Poor Law Union correspondence, workhouse staff registers and administrative records. The guide to poverty and the Poor Laws is a good starting point: www.nationalarchives.gov.uk/help-with-your-research/research-guides/poverty-poor-laws.

Workhouses employed a variety of staff including masters, matrons, medical officers, nurses, dentists, chaplains, teachers, porters, cooks, clerks and many more. TNA's series MH9 has workhouse staff registers from 1837–1921 and these include full names, dates of service, reasons for resignation, salaries and allowances. Series MH12 contains Poor Law Union correspondence, which includes details of paupers and workhouse staff.

BNA has copies of the *Poor Law Unions Gazette,* a weekly newspaper that ran from 1856-1903 and published details of paupers who had deserted their families. Find out more at www.britishnewspaperarchive.co.uk/titles/poor-law-unions-gazette.

To find out more about the history of workhouses, visit www.workhouses.org.uk. As well as capturing the grim reality of daily life in the workhouse, the site also has a wealth of information about the Poor Laws, workhouse locations, Poor Law Unions, workhouse memories, an online museum, timeline, glossary and details of records and resources.

CRIMINAL ANCESTORS

Poverty and fear of the workhouse drove many to crime, from poaching, vagrancy and petty thieving to rioting, vandalism and highway robbery. The agricultural writer and campaigner Arthur Young, in *General View of the Agriculture in Oxfordshire* (1813), noted that Wychwood Forest was 'filled with poachers, deer-stealers, thieves, and pilferers of every kind: offences of almost every description abound so much, that the offenders are a terror to all quiet and well-disposed persons'.

By the dawn of the nineteenth century, many agricultural labourers were destitute due to a combination of poor harvests, the economic depression brought about by the Napoleonic Wars and land enclosures. As the Industrial Revolution gathered pace, increasing mechanisation reduced the need for manual labour and large numbers of people migrated to towns looking for employment, often finishing up living in small, damp, dark and overcrowded homes with inadequate sanitation, resulting in cholera and smallpox epidemics.

Inevitably, there was widespread civil unrest. The enclosure and drainage of open marshlands at Otmoor, where for centuries local inhabitants had grazed sheep, cattle and horses, and reared ducks and geese, led to the infamous Otmoor Riots of 1830. Mobs of agricultural labourers descended on the area night after night, armed with pitchforks, billhooks and other tools of their trade, and destroyed the hated fences, hedges and trees in an attempt to reclaim their ancient rights. Eventually, the Oxfordshire Yeomanry arrived to quell the riots. Around forty rioters were arrested and carted off to Oxford Gaol. However, as they entered Oxford, angry mobsters attacked the cavalry and the prisoners escaped.

In 1898, the Reverend Samuel Crawley, the Rector of Oddington, recalled the Otmoor riots in the Islip Rural Deanery magazine, commenting that 'the inhabitants were unjustly deprived of their rights of free pasturage – a sad pity'.

Not all criminals were driven by poverty. One of Oxfordshire's most notorious criminals, Mary Blandy was the daughter of wealthy attorney and town clerk Francis Blandy of Henley-on-Thames. When Blandy tried to prevent his daughter from marrying Scottish army captain William Cranston, Mary poisoned him with arsenic. She was hanged at Oxford Gaol on 6 April 1752 after spending six months in prison in relative comfort, as befitted a woman of her social standing.

Other inmates were not so fortunate. Conditions in the prison were grim, and many incarcerated there faced public execution or transportation for crimes as diverse as murder, treason, highway robbery, house-breaking, theft, sheep-stealing, arson and forgery. The last man hanged at Oxford Gaol was 23-year-old Oliver Butler, an aluminium worker from Banbury, who was found guilty of murdering his lover, 21-year-old Rose Meadows. Despite doubts about his conviction, he was sent to the gallows on 12 August 1952.

Oxford Castle was used as a prison until 1996. © Nicola Lisle

Local records

The OHC has records for Oxford Prison (O29), which include nominal roll books, index of prisoners' names, records of corporal punishments, medical reception books, hospital occurrence books, records pertaining to individual inmates, registration papers, calendars of prisoners, register of baptisms and burials in the prison 1799–1952, register of executions 1892–1952, and other papers such as correspondence, financial records, minutes, inspection reports, governors' journals and plans.

Quarter Sessions reports (QS1831–QS1856) include various documents relating to prisoners and the judiciary. The most useful is the Calendar of Prisoners, which lists all prisoners awaiting trial at the Quarter Sessions (with name and offence) and those who have been tried (with verdict and sentence). Other records include minute books, appeals and various related documents.

Petty sessions (PS1–PS8) were held from 1828 for minor crimes and civil matters. Under the Magistrates' Courts Act of 1952, they could also try juvenile cases and other minor indictable offences.

OHC's records can be found in the online and searchroom catalogue within the Bampton East, Bampton West, Bullingdon, Henley, Watlington and Henley Borough divisions and within the Oxford City Police Court (PS1–PS8), and include minute books, depositions, lists of minor convictions and fines, individual appeals and administrative papers.

County courts existed from 1846 to deal mainly with civil cases related to finance, property and trusts as well as some probate matters, divorce and care of infants. Each of Oxfordshire's county courts covered an area roughly the same as the Poor Law Unions. The catalogue is online and in the searchroom (CCT1–CCT7) and includes minute books, bankruptcy proceedings, records of summonses, compensation registers, Deeds of Arrangement indexes, correspondence and much more.

Local newspapers carried reports of crimes and court cases; use Heritage Search to locate relevant records.

BSP has published transcriptions relating to prison employees, coroners' inquests, workhouse records, poor relief and Oxford Gaol prisoner portraits, and these are available at the OCL. Some of these publications may also be available in other county libraries.

National records

TNA holds records for the Oxford Circuit of the Assize court, which dealt with serious crime such as murder, arson and robbery. These include details such as the full name of the accused, details of charges, plea, verdict and sentence. The main series are ASSI 2–ASSI6, ASSI 10 and PRO 30/80, which include Crown minute books, indictment files, criminal dispositions and case papers and miscellanea from 1627–1971. For medical and probation reports for 1952–57, see ASSI89. There are some gaps in the records, particularly indictment papers from the 1920s, which were destroyed by enemy action during the Second World War. Records are subject to closure periods of thirty, seventy-five or 100 years.

TNA's criminal registers for England and Wales 1792–1892 are held in series HO26 and HO27, and can be searched on Ancestry. Records give the criminal's name, age, birthplace (rare after 1802), crime, when and where tried, sentence and date of execution or release. For more information and links, see the TNA's guide www.nationalarchives.gov.uk/help-with-your-research/research-guides/criminals-and-convicts.

There are many more series at TNA relating to prisoners, criminal petitions, criminal entry books and other records. Details vary but include any of the following: criminal's full name, aliases, birth year, age, place of birth, residence, occupation, court and location, sentence type and duration, title information, session commencing month and day. Some have photographs, together with a physical description, character description, marital status, newspaper cuttings, petitions for pardons and correspondence. These records can be searched at Findmypast; see TNA guide www.nationalarchives.gov.uk/help-with-your-research/research-guides/crime-prisons-punishment-1770-1935 for information and links.

If your ancestor was one of the many criminals sentenced to transportation, the TNA has records of those transported to Australia from 1787–1879 in series HO10, HO11 and CO 209/7. These include convict censuses, musters, pardons and tickets of leave, and are searchable online at Ancestry. See TNA's guide www.nationalarchives.gov.uk/help-with-your-research/research-guides/criminal-transportation.

Note that before 1776 convicts were transported to North America and the West Indies, but few records have survived.

Another very useful site is Black Sheep Ancestors (www.blacksheepancestors.com), where you can search prison and convict records, execution records and court records.

Finally, the website Our Criminal Ancestors (www.ourcriminalancestors.org) was launched in April 2018 and includes timelines tracing the history of crime, punishment, police and the courts, together with stories from the archives and detailed advice on tracing criminal ancestors.

POLICE

Oxfordshire was served by the Oxfordshire Constabulary from 1857 and the Oxford City Police from 1869. Following the Police Act 1964, both were amalgamated with the Berkshire, Buckinghamshire and Reading Borough forces to form the Thames Valley Constabulary, which was officially created on 1 April 1968. The force was later renamed the Thames Valley Police.

Many of the early records for regional forces have not survived. The OHC has some duty attendance and report books in the Petty Sessions collection (PS/7), as well as various reports, correspondence, character references and other papers in the Borough (BOR) and Quarter Sessions (QS) collections. There is a larger collection for the Oxford City Police (POL1), which includes operational and administrative records, police committee reports and papers of the Oxford City Police Federation and Old Comrades' Association. The BOD also holds records for the Oxford City Police (http://ox.libguides.com/modern-sc/oxford), as the force came under the administrative jurisdiction of the University during the nineteenth century. Note that crime records are closed for 100 years, and personnel records for seventy-five years.

Reports of crimes in local newspapers usually name police officers involved; newspapers will also carry other police-related news and obituaries. Use OHC's Heritage Search to see if your ancestor is mentioned.

BSP has published transcriptions of registers relating to the Oxfordshire Constabulary, Oxford City Police, Banbury constables, special constables, women patrols and jury lists, and these can be found at OCL. Some may also be available at other county libraries.

The Police Roll of Honour Trust (www.policememorial.org.uk) lists police constables and officers who have died in service. The index is organised by police force; the Thames Valley roll of honour includes officers from all of the former constituent forces. Entries appear in date order.

For general background to policing in the UK, together with

details of useful websites, books and journals, visit the Police History Society (www.policehistorysociety.co.uk).

PLACES TO VISIT

Oxford Castle Unlocked

Used as a prison until 1996, Oxford Castle reopened as a visitor attraction ten years later. Costumed guides take you on a tour of the Saxon St George's Tower, the 900-year-old crypt, the eighteenth-century Debtors' Tower and Prison D Wing, and the mound of the eleventh-century motte-and-bailey castle. Other parts of the castle have been transformed into cafés and restaurants, and there are various events on throughout the year. The gift shop stocks books about the castle as well as other souvenirs. www.oxfordcastle unlocked.co.uk

Thames Valley Police Museum

This small museum at the Thames Valley Police Training Centre in Sulhamstead, near Reading in Berkshire, has displays relating to the history of the force and the five former constituent forces. Items include uniforms, equipment, medals, scenes of crime evidence, and artefacts from the Great Train Robbery of 1963 and the case of notorious baby farmer Amelia Dyer. The museum holds very few service records, but is good for getting a feel for life in the local police forces. At the time of writing, the Sulhamstead building has been closed for refurbishment and a reduced collection will be on display at a temporary location in Theale until 2019 or 2020. Keep an eye on the website for updates. www.thamesvalley.police.uk/about-us /who-we-are/thames-valley-police-museum

FURTHER READING

Medical history and ancestry

Harris, Martin J., *Nuffield Orthopaedic Centre: A Pictorial History*, Nuffield Orthopaedic Centre NHS Trust, 2011

Higgs, Michelle, *Tracing Your Medical Ancestors*, Pen & Sword, 2011

Trueta, J., *Gathorne Robert Girdlestone*, Oxford University Press, 1971
Wheeler, Ian, *Fair Mile Hospital: A Victorian Asylum,* The History Press, 2015

Poor laws and paupers

Burlison, Robert, *Tracing Your Pauper Ancestors*, Pen & Sword, 2013
Cole, Anne, *Poor Law Documents Before 1834*, Federation of Family History Societies, 2000
Fowler, Simon, *Poor Law Records for Family Historians*, Family History Partnership, 2011
Hawkings, David T., *Pauper Ancestors*, The History Press, 2011
Paley, Ruth, *My Ancestor was a Bastard: A Family Historian's Guide to Sources for Illegitimacy in England and Wales*, Society of Genealogists, 2004
Raymond, Stuart, *My Ancestor was an Apprentice*, Society of Genealogists, 2010
Thompson, Kathryn, *Apprenticeship and Bastardy Records*, Historical Association, 1997

Criminal ancestors

Hawkings, David T., *Criminal Ancestors*, The History Press, 2009
Wade, Stephen, *Tracing Your Criminal Ancestors*, Pen & Sword, 2009

Police history and ancestry

Haliday, Gaynor, *Victorian Policing*, Pen & Sword, 2017
Shearman, Anthony, *My Ancestor was a Policeman: How Can I Find Out More About Him?*, Federation of Family History Societies, 2000
Stallion, Martin and Wall, David, *The British Police: Forces and Chief Officers 1829–2012*, Police History Society, 2011
Wade, Stephen, *Tracing Your Police Ancestors*, Pen & Sword, 2009

Other

Young, Arthur, *General view of the agriculture of Oxford*, Sherwood, Neely & Jones, 1813

Chapter 5

AGRICULTURAL INDUSTRIES

As a largely rural county, Oxfordshire developed a strong farming tradition that dominated right up to the start of the twentieth century. As late as 1842, James Barclay noted in his *Complete and Universal English Dictionary* that 'the soil, though various, is fertile in corn and grass... [Oxfordshire] has no manufactures of any account, being chiefly agricultural'.

Arable and sheep farming brought prosperity to the county, spawning major textile and brewing industries that sustained Oxfordshire's economy for centuries. Glove-making flourished in Oxford, Woodstock, Burford, Witney and Bampton from the thirteenth century; Cotswold sheep and deer from Wychwood Forest ensured a steady supply of skins, which were tanned and dyed before being turned into gloves and other leather goods. Woodstock became particularly famous for the quality of its gloves, supplying royalty, the aristocracy and the military for several hundred years. The industry declined in the nineteenth century as leather gloves began to go out of fashion.

Oxfordshire's chief textile industry was cloth weaving, which became renowned worldwide.

THE COTSWOLD WOOL TRADE

Cloth-weaving has existed in Oxfordshire since at least the twelfth century, particularly on the western edge of the county and in the north. Cotswold sheep have been bred by Oxfordshire farmers for their long, fine wool for hundreds of years, with the limestone hills

Women working in the machine room at Industrial Gloves (Cheam) Ltd, Woodstock, 1963. © Oxfordshire County Council, Oxfordshire HIstory Centre, Ref. D016339a

and the River Windrush providing a natural source for processing the cloth and powering the fulling mills.

Oxford enjoyed a thriving wool trade during the reign of King John and briefly became one of England's chief cloth-making towns with its own weavers' guild and fulling mills. Oxford's weaving days were relatively short-lived, however, and despite a brief revival in the fourteenth century eventually faded into obscurity. In other parts of the county, though, the trade was flourishing.

By the fifteenth century, Cotswold wool was at the heart of England's burgeoning wool trade with Europe. In Oxfordshire, the industry was centred around the towns of Burford, Chipping Norton and Witney, where wealthy wool merchants have left their mark in the form of resplendent manor houses and churches. Headstones in churchyards were often engraved with cloth-making tools, or

St Mary's Parish Church, Witney, one of the Cotswold 'wool' churches. © Nicola Lisle

featured the distinctive 'bale tombs' thought to be unique to the Windrush Valley.

For centuries cloth-making was largely a cottage industry, with whole families involved, until the appearance of mills and the introduction of the factory system in the early nineteenth century.

Witney blankets

Oxfordshire's earliest and most significant wool-based industry was the Witney blanket trade, which prospered for around 300 years and survived well into the twentieth century.

By the seventeenth century, Witney blankets were regarded as the finest in England and were being regularly exported to North America and Africa. The industry received a major boost when the Hudson Bay Trading Company (established 1670) began placing regular orders. In 1677, historian Dr Robert Plot (1640–96), the first Keeper of the Ashmolean Museum in Oxford, noted that Witney blankets were 'esteemed so far beyond all others that this place has engrossed the whole trade of the Nation for this Commodity', and that around 3,000 people were employed in the industry, 'from eight years old to decrepit old age'.

The first trade guild, the Witney Blanket Weavers' Company, was formed in 1711 and granted a Royal Charter by Queen Anne, giving the industry some much-needed regulation. A Blanket Hall was built in Witney's High Street in 1721, and all completed blankets had to be taken there for inspection before distribution to ensure a consistently high quality.

The dawn of the Industrial Revolution, together with the arrival of the railway in Witney in 1861, gradually transformed the industry, ushering in a new period of prosperity. Mechanisation took place gradually throughout the nineteenth century, while the railway enabled quick and easy importing of coal to the mills and cheap exportation of the finished blankets. Other innovations included the introduction of shift working in the factories.

Witney Blanket Hall – blankets were weighed and inspected in this room. © Nicola Lisle and reproduced by kind permission of Witney Blanket Hall.

Child labour was used extensively in the early nineteenth century, and both women and children worked long hours. In 1874, the maximum number of hours they could work was lowered to ten, with children under fourteen only allowed to work for half a day. Pay was low, with workers being paid according to the amount of cloth produced rather than by the number of hours worked. This archaic practice persisted until the 1950s.

The work was also hazardous as it involved heavy, fast-moving machinery, and losing fingers was not uncommon. Noise was another problem; the combined clatter of seventy or so looms working in unison was so loud that workers had to communicate by lip-reading and sign language, and many ended up profoundly deaf. There was also the danger of catching anthrax, which could be carried into the mills in the wool of infected animals. It was usually fatal, but fortunately instances of it were rare.

One of the greatest dangers, though, was fire, and several major blazes were recorded at Witney's mills over the years, usually caused by the mix of the oil used on the machines and the candles and lamps that provided the lighting during the eighteenth and nineteenth centuries.

Mill workers lived in rows of purpose-built stone houses in the town, for which they had to pay a rent, and they were small and dark, with shared toilets and wells. Most have long since been demolished.

Children rarely went to school as they needed to work to bring in much-needed money for the family. In the late seventeenth century, local cloth and wool merchant William Blake, of Cogges Manor, attempted to rectify the situation by building three schoolhouses in and around Witney. In 1833, the Factory Act decreed that child workers should have at least two hours' of schooling each day, which prompted the foundation of a number of denominational and non-denominational schools in Witney. A government report of 1848, part of a national enquiry into the living conditions of loom workers, found that education was 'more attended to in Witney than in many other large towns of the region'.

At the beginning of the nineteenth century, the industry was dominated by the Marriott, Collier and Early families. By the end of the century this had dwindled to just two, the Earlys and the Smiths.

The Early family had been operating several businesses in Witney from the late seventeenth century. In 1862, Charles Early (1824–1912) inherited his father's firm and gradually bought up other Early sites to amalgamate them all into a single business, Charles Early & Co. His main rival, William Smith (1815–1875), had ironically worked for one of the Early businesses before founding his own firm, William Smith & Co., in the 1850s. Based at Bridge Street Mill, his firm was the first to use the steam engine in the manufacture of blankets. Both men are now regarded as two of the industry's greatest entrepreneurs, and blue plaques were unveiled in their honour in 2009.

The twentieth century marked the gradual decline of the blanket industry. During the Second World War, some mills focused on making blankets for the war effort, while others closed. The introduction of new machinery brought about a revival in the 1950s, but eventually the industry was unable to compete with cheaper goods from the north of England and overseas. The popularity of the duvet in the latter half of the twentieth century, the closure of the railway in Witney in 1970 and the widespread use of central heating after the 1980s all contributed to its demise. The last mill to close was Early's Witney Mill in 2002.

Chipping Norton tweed

Chipping Norton became famous for producing high-quality tweed cloth at its woollen mills during the eighteenth and nineteenth century. The industry was established by William Bliss and run by successive generations of the Bliss family for around 150 years. The first mill was a converted malthouse, purchased in 1804 and known as the Upper Mill, while an old flour mill became the Lower Mill and was converted into a water mill for fulling and spinning.

The company's fortunes were boosted by the arrival of the railway in Chipping Norton in 1855, and both mills were enlarged and modernised to accommodate up-to-date machinery. By the 1880s, the company had an annual turnover of £260,000 and was the largest employer in the town with a workforce of more than 700. The Bliss family had a reputation for being good employers, and received a gold medal for good industrial relations at the Paris Exhibition of 1867.

Tragedy struck in 1872 when Lower Mill was destroyed by fire, with the loss of three lives. Its replacement, built the following year, was designed by Bolton architect George Woodhouse, who also designed some of the cotton mills in Lancashire.

Business began to decline in the late 19th century as the company struggled to compete with overseas manufacturers and with the colourful Scottish tartans that had become the vogue. Upper Mill closed in 1893, with the loss of nearly half the workforce. Soon afterwards the Bliss family relinquished control to the Metropolitan Bank, which lacked its predecessors' caring attitude and became embroiled in a bitter industrial dispute that lasted from 1913-14.

During the First World War the company was involved in manufacturing khaki for soldiers' uniforms, but afterwards went into steady decline, closing in 1980. Lower Mill was converted into luxury apartments in the 1990s and is a distinctive local landmark.

Banbury plush weaving

Plush weaving was the main industry in Banbury and its surrounding villages for over 100 years.

Banbury had a thriving wool trade from around the thirteenth century, on the strength of which it was granted a borough charter in 1554 and a weekly wool market charter in 1608. The former entitled the town to its own Mayor and Corporation. Banbury's luck turned when a fire destroyed a large part of the town in 1628, its castle (no longer extant) was besieged during the Civil War and a plague epidemic broke out in October 1644. For much of the seventeenth century there was widespread poverty.

As the eighteenth century dawned, though, a new industrial town was emerging, at the centre of which was a major textile industry. Initially this was dominated by the manufacture of horse livery and blankets, which were made from a variety of woollens, worsteds and cottons. From this evolved, in the 1740s, a new type of fine-quality cloth, initially known as shag and later as plush. The basic fabric was made from worsted – a fine, smooth woollen yarn – and interwoven with silk or mohair to create a fabric similar to velvet. This was widely

Banbury was at the centre of the wool and plush weaving trades for several hundred years. © Nicola Lisle

used to make clothing, such as waistcoats and hats, but in the 1830s presses were introduced to create embossed upholstery fabric.

In the early days the hand weavers and their families worked from home, and the industry quickly radiated out from Banbury to surrounding villages such as Shutford, Bloxham, Bodicote, Drayton and Chaccombe. One of the earliest plush weaving firms in the area was established in Shutford by Thomas Wrench in 1747, and this turned the village into the largest plush weaving centre after Banbury. Wrench's survived until 1948, outlasting all the Banbury weaving firms.

The arrival of the Oxford Canal in 1778 was a major boost to the trade, allowing cheap and easy import of coal and export of completed goods. Banbury plush became world famous, and was exported to Portugal, Spain, Italy, Russia and Persia (now Iran).

Plush weaving peaked during the early years of the nineteenth century, when it was dominated by Banbury firms such as R. & T. Baughan, and Gillett, Lees & Co., and there were more than 400 looms in operation in the town. By the 1850s the industry was in decline as it struggled to cope with competition from the Midlands and the north. Some local weavers moved to Coventry and other towns where weaving was thriving. The 1841 census recorded 170 plush weavers in Banbury, accounting for about two-thirds of all plush weavers in England; by the 1861 census this number had dropped to less than sixty. By the turn of the century most of the weaving firms had closed. The last to survive was Cubitt's, which still had fourteen working hand looms during the 1890s, but closed in 1909. The firm's equipment was acquired by Wrench's of Shutford.

Relics of the plush trade can be seen in Banbury Museum, including a hand loom and other items from Shutford as well as oral history recordings.

BREWING

Brewing in Oxfordshire was popular from at least as far back as the Middle Ages, the county's fertile soil making it ideal for growing hops and grains. In the early days, brewing was mostly carried out in people's homes, local inns, monasteries and the Oxford colleges. Small independent breweries began to appear in Oxford around the twelfth century, but they struggled to compete with the college breweries.

Large-scale commercial brewing in the county began in the eighteenth century, mainly in Oxford, Witney, Banbury, Henley-on-Thames and the former Berkshire town of Abingdon. One of the earliest breweries was Morland's, which was founded in West Ilsley,

Berkshire, in 1711 by farmer John Morland who sold his beers to public houses in London. During the latter half of the nineteenth century, Morland's moved to Ock Street in Abingdon and acquired most of the town's other breweries. The company was sold to Greene King in 2000, after nearly 300 years of brewing.

Another early brewery was James Clinch's Eagle Brewery in Witney, which was founded in 1811 and prospered for the next 120 years. During that time the company acquired seventy-two public houses in the county, fourteen of which were in Witney. In 1890 Clinch's took over the Blanket Hall Brewery, which had been founded in 1844 by wool manufacturers William Smith and Edward Early. Clinch's was sold to Courage in 1961, but brewing ceased there two years later. In 1982 the site was taken over by Wychwood Brewery.

In 2002, Wychwood bought the original brewing equipment from Brakspear Brewery in Henley-on-Thames, where it had been the town's main brewery since the early eighteenth century.

Several breweries flourished in Oxford during the eighteenth and nineteenth centuries, the main ones being Morrell's (established 1743) and Hall's (established 1795). Morrell's was founded as the Lion Brewery by Richard Tawney, but was eventually taken over by the Morrell family of Headington Hill Hall after Tawney went into partnership with Mark and James Morrell in 1782. Morrell's thrived throughout the nineteenth century, and the Lion Brewery underwent constant expansion and redevelopment. The brewery closed in 1998.

Hall's Oxford Brewery had its origins in the sixteenth-century Swan's Nest Brewery (later Swan Brewery) in Paradise Street, which enjoyed a thriving trade both locally and with London. In the late eighteenth century the brewery was owned by alderman and mayor Sir John Treacher, who sold the company to William Hall in 1795. Hall and his successors continued to expand the business, acquiring numerous other breweries both in Oxford and elsewhere in the county. In December 1896 the brewery became a limited company and changed its name to Hall's Oxford Brewery. Just thirty years later, Hall's was taken over by Samuel Allsopp & Sons, who moved the business out of the county.

Brewing thrived in Banbury during the nineteenth century, with the number of breweries in the town increasing from three to fourteen and several others opening in the surrounding towns and villages. A brewery was established at Hook Norton by John Harris in 1849 and is still operating in the original Victorian tower building. The late nineteenth-century steam engine is still in occasional use, and beer is still delivered to the village in a horse-drawn dray.

FINDING TEXTILE AND BREWERY ANCESTORS

You can verify whether your ancestor worked in the textile or brewing trades by consulting birth, marriage and death certificates. These will also indicate whether other family members were involved in the same trade, which was common. Textile occupations may be given simply as 'weaver', but others you might come across are 'blanket weaver', 'clothier', 'fuller', 'hand loom weaver', 'journeyman weaver', 'loom tuner', 'power loom weaver', 'tabber' and 'tucker'. See Chapter 2 for advice on searching the BMD indexes and obtaining certificates.

Census returns, wills, parish registers and poll books are also good ways of confirming your ancestors' trade, and can be searched or consulted at the OHC. Search the 'People' index for obituaries and other news items; business and trade directories are also useful. Oral history recordings are worth a listen to get a feel for the way a company operated and what life was like for its workers.

The OHC also holds records for several of the businesses connected to the local textile and brewing trades. One of the largest collections relates to Early's of Witney (B1), which includes employee records and salary books, as well as financial and administrative records, a company history, details of the company's social activities and trade union records, among others. The collection also includes the records of the Blanket Weavers' Company of Witney (B1/1), which Edward Early purchased in 1847, and those of Marriott & Sons Ltd (B1/7), due to the fact that the Earlys and Marriotts merged in 1960. If you want to delve deeper into the history of the Early family – who were associated with the blanket trade from the late seventeenth century – there is a collection of family papers (F17) and Charles Early's diaries (P13).

There are similar collections for local brewing companies such as Hall's Oxford & West Brewery (B15), Hunt Edmund & Co. of Banbury (B20), Hitchman & Co. of Chipping Norton (B19), Brakspear & Son of Henley (B33) and Morrells of Oxford (B25).

TNA's Discovery catalogue (http://discovery.nationalarchives.gov.uk) is a good way of checking the location of relevant business records, as they may not all be held by OHC. For example, a search for 'Brakspear & Son' revealed that some administrative and legal records are held by the BRO, as they relate to pubs in towns that were formerly part of Berkshire. Others may be held at TNA.

The MRC holds records for several brewers' organisations, including the Country Brewers' Society (1822–1904) and the Brewers' Society (1904–94). Holdings include annual reports, minutes, records relating to membership subscriptions, administrative records, financial records, publicity material and legal matters. https://www2.warwick.ac.uk/services/library/mrc/explorefurther/subject_guides/brewers.

The National Brewing Library at OBUSC (www.brookes.ac.uk/nbl) is the UK's most comprehensive source of information on the history of brewing, and was formed in the late twentieth century from the merger of several national brewing associations. The collection includes several books on brewing history in Oxfordshire and on local brewing firms.

Another excellent resource is The Brewery History Society (www.breweryhistory.com). Among other things, this includes a list of defunct brewery liveries, searchable by county (there are numerous entries for Oxfordshire), as well as links to individual breweries and other useful resources.

The Witney Blanket Story (www.witneyblanketstory.org.uk /wbp.asp) was originally the website for the Witney Blanket Project, which was set up after the closure of the last Early mill in 2002 and included a touring exhibition. The exhibition is no longer running, but the website gives a comprehensive history of the Witney blanket industry including how blankets were made, stories of people associated with the industry, mill buildings around Witney, a gallery of objects and pictures, a glossary and a comprehensive list of further resources.

PLACES TO VISIT

Cogges Manor Farm

This thirteenth-century manor house was owned by successive generations of the Blake family, who were prominent in the local wool trade. The house and farm have been preserved as they were in the Victorian era, and there are regular events and exhibitions. http://www.cogges.org.uk

Hook Norton Brewery

Take a tour of this original Victorian brewery, which features a fully working steam engine, to see how beer is made and then explore the museum to get a feel for the history of this industry. **Wychwood Brewery**, near Witney, also offers tours of the works. www.hooky.co.uk and www.wychwood.co.uk

Vale and Downland Museum

Explore the history of Wantage and the Vale of White Horse – formerly in Berkshire, but part of Oxfordshire since 1974 – and get a glimpse into town life of the eighteenth and nineteenth century. The library houses around 1,500 books, pamphlets and periodicals and over 100 maps dating from the late eighteenth century to the present. The website includes links to local history articles. http://wantage-museum.com

Waterperry Rural Life Museum

Displays include a collection of tools used by brewers, coopers, farriers, blacksmiths and gamekeepers, as well as domestic items. There are regular events, exhibitions and courses, plus a shop and tea room. www.waterperrygardens.co.uk

Witney Museum

This small but well-stocked museum has displays relating to the blanket industry, including a working loom, as well as archives that include records relating to the Early family. The museum also has displays relating to the local brewing and glove-making industries, life in Witney during the two world wars, and more. www.witneyhistory.org/witneymuseum.html

The Witney Blanket Hall

Built in 1721 by the Company of Blanket Makers, this was where local merchants brought their blankets to be inspected, weighed and measured up until 1845. After that it had various uses, including as a brewery and a lemonade factory. Since 2015 it has been open to the public for guided tours, talks and other events, and as a woollens shop and café.

FURTHER READING

Allen, Brigid, *Morrells of Oxford: The Family and their Brewery 1743–1993*, Oxfordshire Books, 1994

Bond, James and Rhodes, John, *The Oxfordshire Brewer*, Oxfordshire Museum Services, 1985

Brown, Jonathan, *Tracing Your Rural Ancestors*, Pen & Sword, 2011

Brown, Mike, *Oxon Brews: The Story of Commercial Brewing in Oxfordshire*, Brewery History Society, 2004

Teasdale, Vivien, *Tracing Your Textile Ancestors*, Pen & Sword, 2009

Woolley, Rob, *Brewed in the Traditional Manner: The Story of Hook Norton Brewery*, Rewin Books, 2015

Chapter 6

TRANSPORT AND INDUSTRY

Although a largely rural county for much of its existence, Oxfordshire began to develop non-agricultural industries from the early nineteenth century, from manufacturing to printing, retail, finance and scientific research. The decline in the agricultural workforce and the development of urban-based industries saw increased movement towards the towns, which were gradually transformed by the building of more shops and housing. Many of Oxford's most

The White Horse and Blackwell's Bookshop, Broad Street, Oxford, 1910. © Oxfordshire County Council, Oxfordshire History Centre Ref. D269261a

famous retail names emerged during the nineteenth century, such as university outfitters Shepherd and Woodward (1845) and Blackwell's Bookshop (1879), while Boswell's appeared as early as 1738 and is believed to be the world's oldest family-run department store.

Transport has been integral to these industrial and domestic reforms, with the local roads, canals, rivers and railways all playing an important role in the development of the county's industries, trades and commerce. For centuries, the River Thames was a major trade route between Oxfordshire and London. Turnpiked roads provided important coaching links to London, Wales, the Midlands and the South West during the eighteenth century, with Burford, Dorchester, Abingdon and Benson becoming major coaching towns. Coaching inns flourished along the coaching route, and coachmaking became a significant trade.

The river and the roads diminished in importance in the late eighteenth century with the arrival of the Oxford Canal and, later, the railway.

The nationalisation of the canals, railways and road haulage firms in 1948, following the Transport Act of 1947, brought them all under the control of the British Transport Commission (BTC). The BTC was abolished by the Transport Act 1962, and its assets and responsibilities taken over by separate public bodies.

CANALS

As industrialisation began to sweep through Britain, the need for a fast, economical and reliable system for transporting cargo became paramount. Roads and rivers were too slow and inconvenient; a new waterway system was needed that was more easily navigable. Gradually the country was criss-crossed by an extensive network of canals that had none of the natural disadvantages of rivers and could be placed where they were most needed. The ability to raise or lower water levels through the lock system was a vital piece of additional flexibility. The age of the canal had arrived.

All canals needed an Act of Parliament to authorise their construction, with further acts sometimes needed to authorise the raising of additional funding. An increasing number of businesses and investors proposed canal schemes, resulting in the construction of over 4,500 miles of canals by the mid-nineteenth century.

The coming of the railways from the 1830s sounded the death knell for the canals, which were unable to compete in terms of speed and efficiency. Investors transferred their interests to the rail companies, and the canal companies began to struggle. Some were taken over by the rail companies, while others fell into disuse.

The impact on the canal workers was huge. Boatmen had their wages cut by the carrier firms, resulting in many selling their homes and living on the boats with their families. Conditions on the boat were often cramped, and the constant travelling meant that the children were poorly educated. The Canal Boat Acts of 1877 and 1884 attempted to remedy the situation by requiring all boats to be registered and introducing regular inspections by the local authorities.

After nationalisation in 1947, the canals were overseen by the Docks and Inland Waterways Executive, which was responsible to the British Transport Commission. The BTC took direct control in 1953 when the Executive was abolished. The British Waterways Board was established in 1963 to take over the assets and responsibilities of the BTC, and this in turn was taken over in England and Wales by the Canal and River Trust in 2012.

The Oxford Canal

The Oxford Canal is one of England's earliest canals, constructed in the late eighteenth century and stretching for 77 miles, twenty-six of which are in Oxfordshire. It starts at Hawkesbury Junction at Bedworth in Warwickshire, where it connects to the Coventry Canal, and ends in Oxford, where it connects to the River Thames. The scheme was instigated by Sir Roger Newdigate, the MP for the University of Oxford from 1750–80, who owned collieries in

Bedworth and Coventry and wanted an efficient means of transporting coal from the Midlands to Oxford and London.

The Oxford Canal Company was authorised by an Act of Parliament on 21 April 1769 and Newdigate was its first chairman. Construction of the canal began at Hawkesbury Junction in September 1769 under the supervision of noted canal engineer James Brindley. The project was hampered by various disputes and financial problems and took twenty years to complete. The canal reached Banbury in 1778, opening officially on 30 March, but further financial difficulties delayed work on the final Banbury–Oxford stretch until 1787, when it proceeded under the direction of Banbury engineer James Barnes.

The final section reached Oxford in 1789 and was officially opened on 1 January 1790. For the next fifteen years, the new canal was one of the busiest and most profitable in Britain, carrying vast quantities of coal, limestone, iron ore, agricultural products and other goods between London and the Midlands. The canal quickly brought prosperity to the area; local coal prices fell sharply, established trades flourished and new industries began to appear.

Oxford was served by a goods wharf and turning basin at Worcester Street and a coal wharf at New Road, both sadly demolished in the 1950s when car manufacturer William Morris – by then Viscount Nuffield – bought the land and built Nuffield College on part of the former canal basin site. The remaining land became the Worcester Street Car Park, and the canal terminus was relocated to Hythe Bridge Street.

In the early nineteenth century coal merchant Henry Ward established a boatyard and a coal wharf at Jericho, which developed into Oxford's first industrial suburb as other merchants were drawn to the area. In 1825, iron founder William Carter moved his business from Summertown to Jericho, setting up the Jericho Iron and Brass Foundry and producing ornamental ironwork and industrial goods. This became the Eagle Ironworks in 1838, later renamed W. Lucy & Co. Jericho also owed its

Canal Warf near Oxford Castle, 1901. © Oxfordshire County Council, Oxfordshire History Centre, Ref. POX0102714

expansion to the arrival of the Oxford University Press in 1825 (see below).

Elsewhere in the county, the village of Lower Heyford grew in importance after a coal wharf was built there in 1787, while Banbury became a centre for boat building and plush weaving after the establishment of a dry dock and two wharves in 1778.

Sadly, Oxfordshire's canal heyday was short-lived. The building of the Grand Junction Canal in 1805 created a more direct route from

The Oxford Canal at Banbury. © Nicola Lisle

the Midlands to London and bypassed the Oxfordshire section completely. Commercial use of the canal south of Napton in Warwickshire fell sharply, its decline further hastened by the arrival of the railways in the 1840s. In contrast, the northern section, between Napton and Bedworth, continued to be commercially viable right up to the 1960s.

A proposal to close the Oxford Canal was rejected by Transport Minister Barbara Castle in the 1960s, and – like many canals in Britain – it has become popular for boating, walking and cycling.

THE BOATMEN'S FLOATING CHAPEL

In the 1830s, local coal merchant and philanthropist Henry Ward (1780–1852) provided a floating chapel for Oxford's bargemen and their families after hearing that they 'never did and never would present themselves at a church in their rough costume' (G.V. Cox, *Recollections of Oxford*, 1838).

The wooden structure was mounted on a former Thames barge and, according to *Berrow's Worcester Journal*, was 'capable of containing from 120 to 140 persons'. The chapel was consecrated in December 1839 and moored near Hythe Bridge. *Jackson's Oxford Journal* described it as 'a very pretty floating chapel in the Egyptian style' with an 'elegant design'.

For nearly thirty years the barge served as both chapel and schoolroom, with the cost of maintenance covered through public subscriptions. Benefactors included 'heads of colleges and other friends' (*Berrow's Worcester Journal*) as well as members of the Ward family and the Oxford Canal Company, which gave a generous annual donation.

The chapel sank early in 1868 and in its place came St Barnabas Church, financed by OUP manager Thomas Combe (1796–1872) on land provided by Henry Ward's youngest son, George (1823–1887).

Finding canal ancestors

The EP has published three volumes relating to the canal industry in Oxfordshire:

- EUR026 The Boat People of Oxford Canal
  Transcriptions of canal boat registers completed by George James Dew, Canal Boat Inspector for Lower Heyford, from 1889 to 1900. Details include date of inspection, boat name and registration number, place and date of registration, name and address of the owner, name and address of the captain and, for

later records, the number of adults and children on board and comments on the condition of the boat.

- EUR133 The Boat People of Oxford Canal Volume 2
  Canal boat register created by the Oxford Regional Authority following the Parliamentary Act of 1877, with boat name and registration number, names of the owner(s) and master, details of the boat's route and cargo, description of the boat and date of registration.
- EUR379 Oxford Canal Miscellany
  Various records issued by the Banbury Urban Sanitary Authority from 1879 to 1907.

The OHC holds records for the Oxford Canal Company (B112), which includes a lock-keeper's journals (B112/J). It is also worth consulting local newspapers for news items and obituaries; business and trade directories are also useful. There are also several oral history recordings. The BOD also holds records relating to the Oxford Canal Company, including accounts, interest books and transfer books for the period 1769–1848 (ref: MSS Dept a 16, b 41-42, c 102-03).

The main archive for Britain's canals is the Waterways Archive at Ellesmere Port, which holds hundreds of documents arranged by company and including company/staff returns, photographs of boats and canal workers and more. Explore the collection online at http://collections.canalrivertrust.org.uk/home, or there is a research service available.

Records for pre-nationalisation canal companies taken over by rail companies are held at TNA under the RAIL series. You will find miscellaneous records for the Oxford Canal Company at RAIL 855 (http://discovery.nationalarchives.gov.uk/details/r/C13043). These include minutes and reports, stock and share registers, waste books (with details of bills, salaries and other disbursements), ledgers, journals, day books, cash books, letter books, letters received, petitions and other documents related to the planning, construction and administration of the canal.

RAILWAYS

The arrival of the Great Western Railway in the early nineteenth century revolutionised Oxfordshire's economy and landscape. The company was founded in Bristol in 1833 and incorporated by an Act of Parliament in 1835, with Isambard Kingdom Brunel appointed as its first engineer. The first stretch of the London to Bristol line reached Maidenhead in 1838, and was extended to Didcot – then still in Berkshire – the following year. Brunel's original vision was to take the line through Abingdon, but, due to local opposition, the line had to be diverted through Radley to Didcot, turning what was once a tiny rural village into a major railway and commuter town.

There was further opposition in 1837 when GWR proposed to extend the line through the centre of Oxford via Iffley village, terminating close to Magdalen Bridge. Local objection to the plan resulted in the bill being defeated in Parliament. A second bill was similarly defeated when the university raised concerns about undergraduates being able to travel to London, where they might indulge in morally dubious behaviour. The Chancellor of the University, Waterloo hero the Duke of Wellington, was reputedly horrified by the idea of 'ordinary' people being able to travel around more easily.

The railway eventually opened in Oxford in June 1844, with the terminus at Grandpont. The current station opened at the eastern end of Botley Road in 1852, and the Grandpont station became a goods-only station, closing twenty years later.

A further network of railway lines developed in the area from the 1850s, including the Oxford, Worcester and Wolverhampton Railway (1852–53), the Watlington and Princes Risborough Railway (1872), the Banbury and Cheltenham Railway (1881), and the Oxford and Rugby Railway, which linked Oxford to Banbury in 1850 but never reached Rugby as originally planned. There were also various branch lines in places such as Wallingford and Faringdon, which provided connections to the main GWR line.

OXFORDSHIRE'S WORST RAIL DISASTER

On Christmas Eve 1874, an express train travelling from Paddington to Birkenhead crashed between Shipton-on-Cherwell and Hampton Gay, near Kidlington, killing thirty-four and leaving many more with horrific injuries. The cause was a faulty tyre on a carriage that had been added at Oxford station to cope with an unusually high number of passengers. As the train picked up speed, both tyre and wheel began to disintegrate and the carriage quickly derailed. Other carriages soon followed, their smashed remains strewn across the railway lines and down the embankment.

Jackson's Oxford Journal reported that 'the shrieks of the wounded, and the wintriness of the scene combined to fix a life-long impression upon those that had the misfortune to be on the spot.'

You can read more about the accident in the Railways Archive (www.railwaysarchive.co.uk), which includes a downloadable PDF of the official report of the accident investigation dated 27 February 1875.

Finding railway ancestors

Before the nationalisation of the railways in 1947, rail services were operated by numerous regional railway companies. Most of their records were subsequently deposited at TNA and now provide a comprehensive and detailed resource, from staff records to administrative, legal and financial documents, technical drawings, plans and much more.

A good place to start is with the TNA research guide to railway workers (www.nationalarchives.gov.uk/help-with-your-research/research-guides/railway-workers), which provides a good overview of the records available with useful links.

Records of most interest to family researchers are the employment records and accident reports. Employment records are wide-ranging and include staff registers, salary registers, attendance logs, complaints files, disciplinary registers, pension records, registers of leavers and joiners, and records of staff associations. There is no central index of railway employees, so it is essential to know which company your ancestor worked for, or at least to have an idea of the geographical region.

For Oxfordshire family researchers, the following series are likely to be of most use.

- RAIL 264: Great Western Railway Company (GWRC) staff records 1835–1962. Includes Register of Clerks, nine volumes, 1835–1910 (RAIL 264/1-RAIL 264/9); memorandum books related to locomotive staff, 1900–1946 (RAIL 264/10-RAIL 264/17); and registers of drivers and firemen, 1841–1885 (RAIL 264/18-RAIL 264/30) and 1940-56 (RAIL 264/493-RAIL 264/522). http://discovery.nationalarchives.gov.uk/details/r/C12452
- RAIL 270: GWRC Register of Accidents and Related Records. Covers accidents 1920–1939 (RAIL 270/1-RAIL 270/20); memoranda, 1842–1845 (RAIL 270/21); register of compensation paid, 1898–1900 (RAIL 270/22); register of workmen's compensation paid, 1906–9 (RAIL 270/23) and up to 1929 (RAIL 20/24-RAIL 270/30); index to accidents to staff, 1911-13, arranged chronologically (RAIL 270/27-RAIL 270/28). http://discovery. nationalarchives.gov.uk/browse/r/r/C12458
- RAIL 555: Oxford & Bletchley Junction Railway Company, 1840–47. Board and committee minutes. http://discovery.national archives.gov.uk/browse/r/r/C12743
- RAIL 556: Oxford & Rugby Railway Company, c.1840–55. Directors' and shareholders' minutes, contract drawings, ledger and cash book. http://discovery.nationalarchives.gov.uk/browse /r/r/C12744
- RAIL 557: Oxford Railway Company. Petitions and proofs of evidence relating to setting up the company, plus directors' and shareholders' minutes 1836–43 and list of shareholders. Proofs of evidence are of particular interest as they are mostly from individuals, including John Early (blanket manufacturer, Witney),

Henry Swann (paper maker, Eynsham), Michael Underhill (grocer, Oxford) and many more. http://discovery.nationalarchives.gov. uk/browse/r/r/C12745
- RAIL 558: Oxford, Worcester & Wolverhampton Railway Company. Deeds, agreements, directors' and shareholders' minutes, contracts, specifications, estimates and plans. http://discovery. nationalarchives.gov.uk/browse/r/r/C12746
- RAIL 1156: Special Collections: Retired Officers' Society 1900–1963. Although not specifically related to Oxfordshire, this collection might be useful if your ancestor was an officer with one of the railway companies. Includes minute books, cash books, photographs of members of the society. http://discovery. nationalarchives.gov.uk/details/r/C13287
- RAIL 1053: Board of Trade Railway Department of Ministry of Transport: Reports and Returns. This series includes a complete run of Board of Trade accident reports from 1853–1975 (RAIL 1053/51-RAIL 1053/161), covering everything from major train crashes to incidents at work involving minor injuries. In addition to details of the accident, each report includes witness statements by railway workers and passengers. http://discovery.national archives.gov.uk/browse/r/r/C194701 ?uri=C194701

There may well be other series of interest, especially if your ancestor was from Oxfordshire but worked out of the area, so it's worth browsing through the different companies.

TNA also provides a link to the Ancestry database for railway employees (http://search.ancestry.co.uk/search/db.aspx?dbid=1728). Records include staff registers, station transfers, pension and accident records, apprentice records, caution books and memoranda. Search by name, date of birth, year of a particular event/incident, station or company, or just browse by company, division or area and year range. You can search free, but you need an Ancestry account to view records or to browse.

The OHC holds some miscellaneous papers relating to the Great Western Railway Company and other local companies (mainly legal and administrative papers, plans and correspondence), as well as photographs and a selection of oral history recordings. Local newspapers and journals may also have details of railway incidents and obituaries of former railway workers.

Finally, the National Railway Museum in York (www.nrm.org.uk), founded in 1975, is one of the UK's largest collections of railway records and memorabilia, covering 300 years of railway history. The records of individuals and families include drivers' diaries, log books, training notes and service papers, as well as papers from railway historians, societies and campaign groups. The museum also holds an archive of Board of Trade accident reports, from 1855 to 2001, which can be viewed in the museum's library or searched online in the Railway Archive (www.railwaysarchive.co.uk/index.php).

The website includes family history advice, useful links and several downloadable resource packs, including *Railway Accidents*, *Women Railway Workers*, *Railway Police and Railway Crimes*, *Railway War Memorials* and both world wars.

There is also a large collection of railway magazines, over 25,000 books, a timetable collection (including Bradshaw's), technical papers and records relating to railway works and companies, a vast collection of photographs from 1850 to the present and other memorabilia.

THE AGE OF INDUSTRY

The transport revolution boosted productivity in the county as first the canals and later the railways made it easier to import raw materials and export finished goods. Manufacturing industries flourished in the county, particularly in Oxford and Banbury, with the latter developing rapidly from a small market town into a major industrial centre.

Oxfordshire was still largely an agricultural county in the

eighteenth and nineteenth century, and there was constant demand for agricultural machinery. There were several ironworks and manufacturers of agricultural machines and implements during the nineteenth century, notably the Oxfordshire Steam Ploughing Company in Oxford (established 1868), the Vulcan Foundry at Neithrop, near Banbury (established 1796) and the Cherwell Iron Works in Banbury (established 1862).

One of the most prominent Oxford firms was W. Lucy & Co., which was a major employer in the city. Its roots were in a modest ironmongery established in Oxford's High Street by William Carter in 1812. Thirteen years later, Carter moved his business to the developing industrial area around the canal at Jericho, renaming it Jericho Iron and Brass Foundry and producing mainly agricultural machinery, decorative ironwork and lamp posts. The company was taken over by Charles Grafton in 1838 and became Eagle Ironworks. After further name changes, it was taken over by Charles Kelley in 1897 and established as W. Lucy & Co., specialising in iron and steel bookcases, library shelving and storage, and notably producing shelving for the Bodleian Library, Cambridge University library and Windsor Castle library. Lucy's association with Oxford came to an end in 2005 when the firm moved to Thame and the Eagle Ironworks building was controversially demolished to make way for modern apartments.

Another major employer was Britannia Works at Fish Street, Banbury, which was established by engineer Sir Bernhard Samuelson in 1848 and quickly gained a reputation for producing a range of good-quality agricultural tools and machinery and introducing the concept of mass production. The firm's output included digging and mowing machines, chaff and linseed cutters, rollers and reapers, and in 1850 won prizes for its turnip top cutter and churn. At the Great Exhibition in 1851, Britannia Works was granted a licence to manufacture the American-patented McCormick reaper, which became one of its most successful products.

It was Britannia Works that transformed Banbury from a modest market town, which relied on weaving, brewing and malting for its livelihood, into a major industrial centre. In Samuelson's obituary in 1905, the *Banbury Guardian* credited him with being Banbury's 'modern founder…who gave the town its industrial character and modern growth'.

The original Fish Street site housed machine and fitters' shops, powered by a two-cylinder steam engine, and was known as the Upper Works. A new site close to the canal became the Lower Works, and was the main focus of the firm's development. In 1870 the two sites were connected by a light tramway, which also connected to the railway station. As the company expanded, demand for labour outstripped supply and Samuelson was forced to recruit from outside Banbury. The result was an influx of people into the town, with the meadows around the River Cherwell disappearing under rows of houses and extra schools being built to cope with the increase in population. Census returns show that the population of Banbury rose by more than 1,500 between 1841 and 1851, an unprecedented increase at that time. A major fire at Britannia Works in 1912 signalled a downturn in the company fortunes, which not even a major restructuring in 1928 could reverse. The company closed in 1933, twenty-eight years after the death of its founder.

Meanwhile, a completely different kind of manufacturing was taking place in Oxford. In 1874, Sarah Cooper, wife of grocer Frank Cooper, produced a batch of marmalade using a surplus stock of Seville oranges, packed it in white, earthenware jars and put it out for sale in her husband's shop at 83–84 High Street. The marmalade became an instant hit with Oxford dons and undergraduates, and before long it was a national favourite, revolutionising the British breakfast, gaining royal approval and finding its way to British embassies all over the world.

Sportsmen were particularly keen on the energizing properties of the tangy, slightly bitter-tasting marmalade, and Frank Cooper cleverly exploited this in his marketing. In 1912, the front cover of

Alden's *Oxford Almanack* featured an advertisement showing a college sportsman holding a megaphone in one hand and a jar of Cooper's marmalade in the other, with the slogan 'Frank Cooper's Oxford marmalade. The marmalade to train on.' The same year, a jar of Cooper's marmalade was included in Captain Scott's rations during his Antarctica expedition, and was discovered buried in the ice many years later.

By the turn of the century, the Coopers had extended their production to jam, sauces and soups, and had taken on extra staff to cope with the increased workload.

In 1903, following the introduction of the Factory and Workshop Act 1901, the Coopers moved production to a purpose-built factory in Park End Street, its close proximity to Oxford Station enabling more efficient delivery of ingredients and distribution of the finished product. The factory was expanded several times during and after the First World War, but it was requisitioned by the Ministry of Food during the Second World War and production moved to the old ice rink in Botley Road (on the site now occupied by Waitrose). The business was taken over by Brown and Polson in 1967 and production was moved briefly to Wantage before being transferred out of the area. Frank Cooper's Oxford is now owned by the Hain Daniels Group.

Cooper's former shop is now occupied by the Oxford Bus Company (No.83) and the Grand Café (No.84). The factory in Park End Street is now a restaurant and bar known as the Jam Factory, and is a listed building.

There were many more Oxfordshire industries, including quarrying, brick manufacture, boat-building, chair-making and bell-founding. Visit www.british-history.ac.uk/vch/oxon/vol2/pp225-227 to find out more.

Industry records

If you know which company your ancestor worked for, use OHC's Heritage Search to locate records in the archive catalogue or business index. There is a collection for Frank Cooper (B3), but there may be items relating to other businesses within other collections. There may also be news items and obituaries in local newspapers, as well as relevant photographs and oral history recordings. Any companies that still exist are likely to have retained their records, so it might be worth contacting them.

TNA's Discovery will indicate relevant records either in its own holdings or in other archives, or you could search its guides www.nationalarchives.gov.uk/help-with-your-research/research-guides/businesses and www.nationalarchives.gov.uk/help-with-your-research/research-guides/business-history-records-held-by-other-archives.

The survival of business records varies greatly, but with luck you might find staff registers, salary registers, disciplinary files, pension records, accident books, details of staff clubs or associations, cash books, minutes and annual reports.

The Museum of Rural Life in Reading (https://merl.reading.ac.uk) has records relating to national agriculture, agricultural manufacturing and engineers as well as related industries.

Finally, don't forget street and trade directories (see Chapter 2) and trade union records at the MRC (see Chapter 1).

PUBLISHING AND THE OXFORD UNIVERSITY PRESS

Bookbinding, parchment/paper-making, printing and publishing firms have existed in Oxford since at least the fifteenth century. One of England's earliest newspapers, *Mercurius Aulicus*, was produced in Oxford during the English Civil War to promote Royalist propaganda and is believed to be the first newspaper to try to influence public opinion, thereby laying the foundation for modern journalism.

Oxford University was involved in the printing trade from the late fifteenth century. After its formation in 1586, Oxford University Press dominated the industry locally, expanding very quickly and obtaining a charter from Charles I in 1636 to print 'all manner of books'. The first print shop was established in the Sheldonian Theatre in 1669 by Dr John Fell, Dean of Christ Church and a

Clarendon Building and Sheldonian Theatre, both formerly used by Oxford University Press before its move to Walton Street. © Nicola Lisle

Delegate of the Press, and moved to the Clarendon Building in Broad Street in 1713.

The Press moved to its current site in Walton Street in 1830, and was partly responsible for the development of the canal-side suburb of Jericho on what was formerly farm land. With generations of local families working for the Press, Jericho became known as the printers' village and was dominated by about a dozen large families.

One well-known local figure was Thomas Combe, who started working for the OUP as superintendent of the learned book division in 1834, eventually rising to the position of Printer of the University. After his marriage to Martha Edwards, the daughter of an Oxford ironmonger, in 1840, he became a major shareholder in the Press, greatly increasing its profits and amassing a considerable personal fortune – much of which he used to build amenities for the growing population of Jericho. St Luke's Chapel (on the old Radcliffe

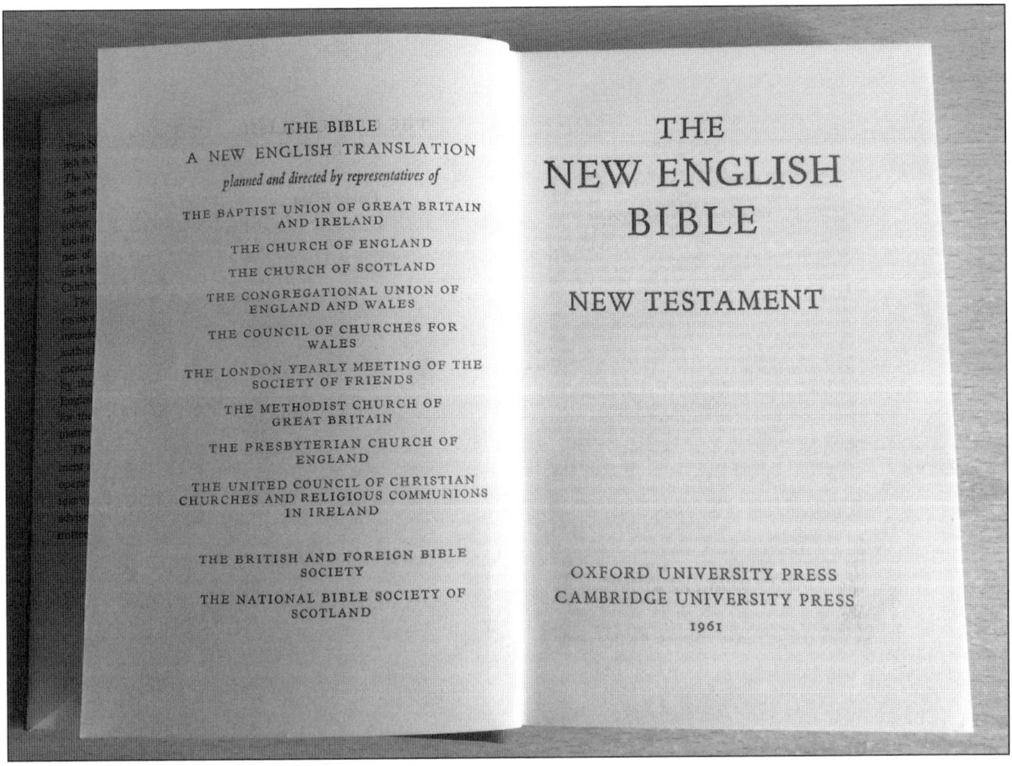
THE BIBLE
A NEW ENGLISH TRANSLATION
planned and directed by representatives of
THE BAPTIST UNION OF GREAT BRITAIN AND IRELAND
THE CHURCH OF ENGLAND
THE CHURCH OF SCOTLAND
THE CONGREGATIONAL UNION OF ENGLAND AND WALES
THE COUNCIL OF CHURCHES FOR WALES
THE LONDON YEARLY MEETING OF THE SOCIETY OF FRIENDS
THE METHODIST CHURCH OF GREAT BRITAIN
THE PRESBYTERIAN CHURCH OF ENGLAND
THE UNITED COUNCIL OF CHRISTIAN CHURCHES AND RELIGIOUS COMMUNIONS IN IRELAND
THE BRITISH AND FOREIGN BIBLE SOCIETY
THE NATIONAL BIBLE SOCIETY OF SCOTLAND
THE NEW ENGLISH BIBLE
NEW TESTAMENT
OXFORD UNIVERSITY PRESS
CAMBRIDGE UNIVERSITY PRESS
1961

New English Bible. © Nicola Lisle, from author's collection

THE NEW ENGLISH BIBLE
New Testament

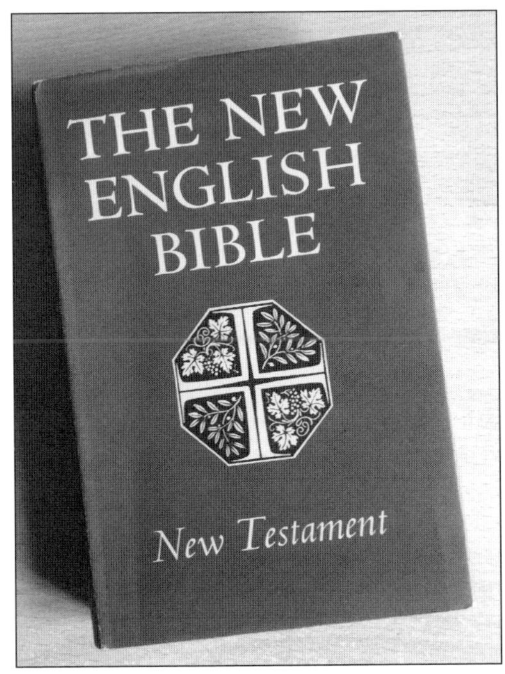

One of the OUP's many specialities was bibles, like this New English Bible from 1961. © Nicola Lisle, from author's collection

Infirmary site, now owned by the University of Oxford) and St Barnabas Church, close to the canal, were both provided by Thomas Combe, and a blue plaque on the church pays tribute to his legacy.

Another key figure at the OUP was Vivian Ridler, the last holder of the post of Printer to the University (1958–78), who modernised the printing process by introducing new techniques and establishing the first fully-mechanised bindery.

The OUP's printing factory closed in 1989, but its publishing operation is now a global enterprise. From early on, the OUP specialised in Bibles, dictionaries, academic books and reference works, some of the most famous titles including the King James version of the Bible and Prayer Book (1675), the *Oxford English Dictionary* (1884–1928), the *Dictionary of National Biography* (acquired in 1917), *The Oxford Atlas* (1951) and *The New Grove Dictionary of Music* (acquired in 2003).

OUP Archive

The OUP archive (https://global.oup.com/uk/archives/index.html) holds some records from the nineteenth century, mainly relating to key figures at the Press, but detailed records don't start until the First World War. Around half of the Press's 700-strong workforce were conscripted shortly after the outbreak of the war, and they are recorded in *On Active Service, War Work at Home 1914–1919* (OUP, 1920). The Roll of Service at the front of the book includes all those who served, with information such as:

- Position at OUP
- Details of any previous positions held at OUP
- Date enlisted
- Regiment and location(s), with dates
- Details of any wounds and hospitalisation, with dates
- Date of discharge or demobilization
- Date returned to OUP, if applicable
- Date and place of death, if applicable.

Forty-four members of OUP staff were killed in action, with another dying of his injuries after his return, and they are remembered with a war memorial in the OUP Quad.

CASE HISTORY
An entry for 'CHAPMAN, H.S.' tells us that he worked as an apprentice in the Composing Room and enlisted with the M.G.C. (Machine Gun Corps) on 16 November 1916. He served in England until 3 April 1917 and crossed to France on that date. He was killed in action in France on 12 May 1917.

The second section of the book, *War Work at Home*, gives an excellent overview of the OUP during the war. As with many companies, women were drafted in to help cover the staff shortfall, and the workers attempted to keep their spirits up by starting an annual Flower and Vegetable Show. If your ancestor worked at the OUP during this time you are unlikely to glean much from this section in the way of personal details, but you will get a good feel for what life was like for staff on the home front and how they contributed to the war effort.

Another excellent resource is the OUP's in-house quarterly magazine, *The Clarendonian*, which ran from January 1919 until the mid-1980s. The magazines are bound into hard-back volumes, each covering three years and each with its own index, making it very easy to look up individuals. Contents include:

- Retirement notices, with dates of service, the section(s) worked in, words of appreciation and comments on involvement in OUP social clubs and sports teams
- News and official notices, such as appointments and promotions, exam results and deaths
- Detailed obituaries (some run to several pages)
- Reports on the activities of OUP clubs and societies
- Reviews of OUP plays and musical shows, with casting details and pictures

- Letters
- Articles on aspects of OUP history.

Finally, an invaluable source – which is also available in public libraries and to buy – is *On the Press: Through the Eyes of the Craftsmen of OUP*, written by Mick Belson, who worked at the OUP from 1958 to 2001 and was the last editor of *The Clarendonian*. The book draws from all issues of *The Clarendonian* as well as the author's own experiences to give a detailed history of the OUP and capture a sense of its family atmosphere. Most importantly, it includes an index so you can easily check whether your ancestor is mentioned.

The most useful chapter for family historians is 'Retirement and Death', which has dates of service, department(s), any certificates or other forms of special recognition, and date of death. Also worth a look is the chapter on clubs and sports, which gives a good flavour of the social life at the OUP. From the late nineteenth century, the Clarendon Press Institute – known affectionately as The Stute – was the focal point for a variety of music, drama, dancing and sports clubs. This is where you might discover that your ancestor had an unsuspected talent!

CASE HISTORY

Search in the index for almost any name, and there's a good chance you will get more than one result – proof that often several generations of local families worked for the Press. A search in the index for 'Green, William', for example, yielded three results. The oldest William worked as an engineer from 1856–1881 and had seven sons, one of whom was also William, and all of whom worked for the Press. One of the sons, Joseph, had three sons who worked for the Press; one of these sons, Lionel, also had a son, Maurice, who was a proofreader. Between them, the family notched up 380 years' service!

CAR MANUFACTURING

Morris Motors

Compared to many other parts of the UK, Oxfordshire was largely untouched by the Industrial Revolution. It was not until the early twentieth century that heavy industry came to the county when William Morris founded his car manufacturing empire in the centre of Oxford. At its peak, the Cowley factory employed 30,000 people and was one of the first employers in Oxfordshire to attract significant numbers of workers from outside the county.

Originally a cycle manufacturer and repairer, who started his own business at his Cowley home as a teenager, by the turn of the century Morris was also repairing motorcycles and was known as Oxford's 'sole maker of the celebrated Morris Cycles and Motor Cycles'. In 1909 he acquired new premises in Longwall Street, just off Oxford's busy High Street, and began to sell, hire and repair motor cars.

At the time, motoring was still largely the preserve of the wealthy. Morris was determined to change that by producing a small, affordable car of good quality that would open up motoring to the masses.

In 1912, he established WRM Motors Ltd at his Longwall Street garage and designed his first car, the Morris Oxford – popularly known as the Bullnose Morris due to its bullet-shaped radiator. The two-seater car was manufactured at the former Oxford Military College in Cowley, and went on sale in 1913. Almost immediately, Morris secured an order of 400 cars from London motor dealer Stewart and Ardern. The following year another popular model, the Morris Cowley, rolled off the production lines.

During the First World War the factory switched to producing munitions, but car production resumed after the war under a new company name, Morris Motors Ltd, which brought together a number of Morris's subsidiary companies and became profitable very quickly. By the mid-1920s, Morris dominated the British car market, alongside Austin and Ford.

The Cowley plant once again became a munitions factory during the Second World War, producing military aircraft, torpedoes and

Morris Motors Body Shop, c. 1920-29. © Oxfordshire County Council, Oxfordshire History Centre, Ref. D271394a

armour-plated shells, as well as assembling American lorries and tanks.

During the post-war years Morris became the largest car manufacturer in Europe and the first to produce a million vehicles. His most famous model of this era was the Morris Minor, which made its debut in September 1948.

The post-war era also saw the company undergoing a series of mergers and takeovers. In 1952, Morris Motors Ltd merged with Austin Rover to form the British Motor Corporation (BMC), with William Morris – by then Lord Nuffield – as its first Chairman. In 1966, three years after Lord Nuffield's death, BMC took over Jaguar to form British Motor Holdings (BMH), which merged with Leyland Motors two years later to become the British Leyland Motor Corporation (BLMC). The various mergers meant that by now the company's output included not only cars but also buses, trucks, milk floats and a wide range of construction equipment, and it had premises in Oxford, Cowley, Reading, Newbury and High Wycombe.

In 1975, the company was nationalised and became British Leyland Ltd (BL). The Cowley factory continued to operate and was still producing some Morris models until 1984, although the main production of the Morris marque was transferred to Birmingham's Longbridge plant in 1982.

In 1986 British Leyland was re-privatised and changed its name to the Rover Group, which then encompassed the Austin Rover Group, Land Rover Group, Freight Rover and Leyland Trucks. From 1988, the Rover Group was owned by British Aerospace, which sold the company to BMW in 1994. BMW now produces the new Mini at Plant Oxford, which was developed on the site of the former Pressed Steel Company (see below) in 2000.

The other former Morris Motors site became the Oxford Business Park, which comprises nearly seventy companies, including the European headquarters of Harley-Davidson Motorcycles, the international headquarters of Oxfam (which was founded in Oxford in 1942), and offices for the Royal Mail, BT, Inland Revenue, British Gas and many more.

EYEWITNESSES

'Pay in those days in the motor industry was better than in most industries. My own pay when I started with the company in 1920 was tuppence halfpenny an hour.' *George Walker, a former general works manager at Morris Motors (OHC Oral History Recording OHOHA: M523)*

'The high wages were definitely the attraction. Not the work, the wages. They were fantastic wages compared to anywhere else... when I was working there I was earning £30 a week at one time, and my wife was working full time at Marks and Spencer for about £7 a week...That's how well paid you were compared to everybody else.' *Mick Morley, who worked on the assembly line at Morris Motors from 1954 (OHC Oral History Recording OXOHA: OT40)*

'It wasn't the nicest place to work...it was hot, uncomfortable and smelly.' *Bill Kelly, who came from Portsmouth to work at Morris Motors in 1958 (OHC Oral History Recording OXOHA: OT40)*

MG Car Company Ltd

In 1923, the Morris Motors sales manager, Cecil Kimber, pioneered a range of sports cars as a promotional sideline, initially using a modified version of the Morris chassis but later developing a purpose-designed chassis. The earliest models carried the official Morris Oxford logo, but in 1928 the MG 14/28 super sports car became the first to bear the famous MG logo when William Morris established the MG Car Company Ltd.

In 1929, production of the MG was moved to Abingdon, taking over some of the sheds formerly used by the Pavlova Leather Company. Kimber continued to produce new designs, including the R-type and Q-type racing cars during the 1930s. Before and after the Second World War, the T-series Midgets became popular and were exported worldwide. In 1935 MG formally became part of Morris Motors Ltd.

MGB on display in Abingdon County Hall Museum. © Nicola Lisle by kind permission of the British Motor Museum, Gaydon, Warwickshire

The MG factory in Abingdon was closed by British Leyland in 1980, with the loss of 1,100 jobs. In just over fifty years, the factory had produced over a million cars.

Pressed Steel Company Ltd

In 1926 Morris helped to establish the Pressed Steel Company, which manufactured car bodies at a factory set up adjacent to the car plant and became another very successful enterprise. The number of employees escalated from just 800 in 1926 to 12,000 in 1953, with an official company advertisement that year boasting of having 'the largest press shops in Europe with over 350 power presses' with 'a factory area at Cowley alone more than half the size of Hyde Park'.

In 1956 another factory was opened in Swindon, followed by one in Linwood, Scotland, in 1961.

Pressed Steel was taken over by the British Motor Corporation in 1965, and became part of all subsequent mergers (see above).

Finding records

The main source is the British Motor Industry Heritage Trust (BMIHT) Archive, which was established in 1983 and is based at the British Motor Museum at Gaydon, Warwickshire. This is a vast archive that encompasses Morris Motors and all its associated companies and mergers as well as those of other manufacturers. The museum's website has a link to the TNA page for BMIHT (http://discovery.nationalarchives.gov.uk/browse/r/h/A13532972), where you can search for records and then request an appointment to view them in the museum's Reading Room.

From the main page, select 'BMIHT Business Records Collection' and then either browse through the companies listed on the right or search for the company you are interested in. Holdings for Morris Motors Ltd include:

- Insurance salaries books, with names of workers and details of contributions, 1919–20

- Wages books, 1920–23
- Accident report book with staff photos, notes and newspaper cuttings, 1937–55
- Monthly salary books, 1940–42
- Deeds of apprenticeships, 1942
- Engagement books, 1947–82
- Left service books, 1947–83
- Transfer books, showing details of staff transfers between departments, 1947–83
- Index book showing names and clock numbers of workers, with starting and leaving dates, 1952–75.

Holdings for the M Company and Pressed Steel are fairly limited, but there are two employee registers for MG from 1927–30 giving names, ages, pay rates and details of any dismissals and redundancies, plus a wages ledger for 1956–74. Records for Pressed Steel mainly give general information about pay rates, notes of pay increases, apprenticeships and staff conditions.

The Nuffield Papers are also worth a browse, although these are largely accounts, corporate records, legal records, strategy and planning papers, minutes of meetings and general correspondence relating to Lord Nuffield's various business interests, as well as his personal papers and photographs.

The OHC holds a large volume of material related to Morris Motors, MG and Pressed Steel, most of which consists of publicity materials, press cuttings, building plans, surveyors' and sanitary inspectors' reports, nominal ledgers and photographs. Some personal papers of former employees have survived in the form of notebooks and scrapbooks with personal recollections, leaflets and cuttings. There are also several oral history recordings. These collections give a good feel for the way the companies operated, the industrial disputes that dogged much of their later existence, and what it was like to work in the factories and offices there.

PLACES TO VISIT

Canals

TOOLEY'S BOATYARD, BANBURY

Established in 1790 to build and repair the horse-drawn wooden canal boats, Tooley's Boatyard is the oldest working boatyard in the country. It was fully restored in the 1990s and includes a 200-year-old blacksmith's forge, 1930s workshops – including a carpenter's store, machine workshop and paint store – and the dry dock, where you can watch work in progress. Tom Rolt's 1944 publication *Narrow Boat*, an account of his voyage from Tooley's Boatyard in 1939, helped raise awareness of the decline of Britain's canals and led to the establishment of the Inland Waterways Association. Rolt is

Tooley's Boatyard, Banbury. © Nicola Lisle

Tooley's Boatyard, Banbury. © Nicola Lisle

commemorated at the boatyard with a blue plaque and the Tom Rolt Bridge. www.tooleysboatyard.co.uk

Banbury Museum

Explore the history of Banbury's canal heritage and how it boosted the local weaving and brewing trades, its development into a market town in the Victorian era and more. Displays include historic costumes from the seventeenth century and a look at Banbury in the Civil War. Changing exhibitions, family activities, shop and café. www.banburymuseum.org

Oxford Canal Heritage Trail

Walk along the Oxford Canal towpath to see preserved wharves and boatyards as well as relics of the canal's heyday. A downloadable

Start of the Oxford Canal towpath at Hythe Bridge Street, Oxford. © Nicola Lisle

trail guide is available from the website of The Oxford Canal Heritage Project. www.oxfordcanalheritage.org

Railways

Didcot Railway Centre

Home of the Great Western Society since 1967, six years after it was formed to preserve GWR heritage. Displays include what is believed to be the largest locomotive collection from a single company in the world, former railway buildings, a recreation of one of Brunel's broad gauge railway lines, a 1932 engine shed, old railway coaches and wagons and more. There is also the Great Western Society museum, photograph collection and archive. There are regular steam and diesel days, gala days and themed events, and a shop and café on site. www.didcotrailwaycentre.org.uk

PENDON MUSEUM

Indoor model railway and landscape capturing the Vale of White Horse in the 1920s and 1930s alongside the 1930s Madder Valley railway and a Dartmoor scene. Shop and regular events. www.pendonmuseum.com

Oxford University Press

OXFORD UNIVERSITY PRESS MUSEUM

Situated next to the Archive, the OUP Museum tells the story of the OUP from its earliest days to the present. Information panels are complemented by displays of old printing equipment, including a nineteenth-century printing press, as well as some of the OUP's most notable publications. Entry is free, but you need to book in advance. https://global.oup.com/uk/archives/5.html

Morris Motors

MORRIS MOTORS MUSEUM, LONG HANBOROUGH

Part of the Oxford Bus Museum since 2004, the Morris Motors Museum tells the Morris story through photographs, drawings and other memorabilia, and has a range of vintage Morris cars and bicycles on display. www.oxfordbusmuseum.org.uk

NUFFIELD PLACE, NEAR HENLEY-ON-THAMES

William Morris bought this early twentieth-century house in 1933 because it was close to Huntercombe golf course, which he had purchased in 1926. When he was created a viscount the following year, he took the title Lord Nuffield. He lived at Nuffield Place with his wife, Elizabeth, until his death in 1963. The rooms have been preserved almost exactly as he left them, and reflect the surprisingly modest tastes of a couple who were by then extremely wealthy. On display are posters, newspaper cuttings and many of the Nuffields' personal possessions. www.nationaltrust.org.uk/nuffieldplace

British Motor Museum, Gaydon

Formerly the Heritage Motor Centre and renamed the British Motor Museum in 2016, the displays include a reconstruction of Morris's Cowley office, laid out exactly as he left it in 1963. There is also a Reference Library, accessible during museum opening hours, and the BMIHT archives (see above). www.britishmotormuseum.co.uk

Museum of Oxford

Displays include a Morris Motors section with old manuals, car badges, lapel badges and a 1933 brochure, as well as a trades union badge, membership card and other personal belongings of former Pressed Steel worker Robert Couling (1908–82). www.museumofoxford.org

Abingdon County Hall Museum

Among the displays in this town centre museum is an MG exhibition, which includes a history of the Abingdon factory, MG memorabilia and the penultimate MGB made in the town before the factory's closure in 1980. There are also model MG cars on display. www.abingdon.gov.uk/partners/abingdon-county-hall-museum

Kimber House, Abingdon

The headquarters of the MG Car Club in Abingdon, adjacent to the former factory, has an exhibition of MG memorabilia, a library, an archive of more than 10,000 photographs and production records for most MG models up to 1950. There is also a small shop. www.mgcc.co.uk

Boundary House, Abingdon

The former home of Cecil Kimber, the creator of the MG marque, is now marked with a blue plaque.

Mini Plant Oxford

Take a guided tour behind the scenes to see how the Mini is produced, and explore the history of car production in Oxford in the exhibition space.
www.visitmini.com

FURTHER READING

Canals

Hood, Nancy, *Oxford Waterways*, Amberley Publishing, 2012
Ware, Michael, *Canals and Waterways*, Shire Publications, 1987
Wilkes, Sue, *Tracing Your Canal Ancestors*, Pen & Sword, 2011

Railways

Drummond, Di, *Tracing Your Railway Ancestors*, Pen & Sword, 2010
Hardy, Frank, *My Ancestor Was a Railway Worker*, Society of Genealogists, 2009
Hawkings, David T., *Railway Ancestors: A Guide to the Staff Records of the Railway Companies of England and Wales 1822-1947*, The History Press, 2008)
Jones, Hugh, *The Chiltern Railways Story*, The History Press, 2010
May, Trevor, *The Victorian Railway Worker*, Shire, 2000
Richards, Tom, *Was Your Grandfather a Railwayman?*, T. Richards, 2002
Simpson, Bill, *A History of the Railways of Oxfordshire Part 1: The North*, Lamplight Publications, 1997
Simpson, Bill, *A History of the Railways of Oxfordshire Part 2: The South*, Lamplight Publications, 2008

Oxford University Press

Belson, Mick, *On the Press: Through the Eyes of the Craftsmen of OUP*, Robert Boyd Publications, 2003
Gadd, Ian, Eliot, Simon and Louis, W. Roger (eds), *The History of Oxford University Press* (three volumes), OUP, 2014

Robbins, Keith (ed.), *History of Oxford University Press Vol. IV 1970–2004*, OUP, 2017

Morris Motors

Bardsley, Gillian and Laing, Stephen, *Making Cars at Cowley: From Morris to MINI*, The History Press, 2013
Carver, Mike, Seal, Nick and Youngson, Anne, *British Leyland Motor Corporation 1968–2005: The Story from the Inside*, The History Press, 2015
Hayter, Don, *MGB Story: The birth of the MGB in MG's Abingdon Design and Development Office*, Veloce Publishing Ltd, 2012
Hull, Peter, *Lord Nuffield: An Illustrated Life of William Richard Morris, Viscount Nuffield, 1877–1963*, Shire Publications, 1993

Other

Allen, Brigid, *Cooper's Oxford: A History of Frank Cooper Ltd*, Archive Services of Oxford, 1979
Bleay, Hazel *Memories of Bygone Oxford Shops*, Robert Boyd Publications, 2010
Clark, Ted, *Banbury History and Guide*, Sutton, 1992
Graham, Malcolm, *Banbury Then and Now*, The History Press, 2011
Potts, William, revised and edited by T. Clark, *A History of Banbury*, Gulliver Press, 1978
Woolley, Liz, *Oxford's Working Past: Walking Tours of Victorian and Edwardian Industrial Buildings*, Huxley Scientific Press, 2012
Trinder, Barry, *Victorian Banbury*, Phillimore, 1982

Chapter 7

EDUCATION

OXFORD UNIVERSITY

For centuries Oxford has been defined by its university, which dates back to at least 1096 and is the oldest English-speaking university in the world. Visitors to Oxford are sometimes confused by the fact that there is no central university campus. This is because Oxford University, like Cambridge, is made up of individual colleges and faculties, which were established in a fairly haphazard fashion over several hundred years.

The university probably originated from early gatherings of clerical and monastic scholars in the city some time during the eleventh century, and this gradually developed into a recognised organisation. The title of Chancellor was first conferred in 1214, and the university was granted a royal charter by Henry III in 1248.

Medieval students and academics lived in lodgings around the town, with lectures taking place in hired premises, but in the mid-thirteenth century the first colleges began to appear, endowed by private benefactors. The earliest was University College, founded in 1249 by William of Durham, followed by Balliol in 1263 and Merton in 1264. Today there are thirty-eight colleges, six Permanent Private Halls (PPHs) and numerous academic departments.

The university enjoyed its most rapid period of growth from the nineteenth century, with an ever-expanding curriculum, the awarding of a greater range of degrees, fellowships and doctorates, and an increasing emphasis on research. The greatest innovation, though, was the gradual integration of women into the university in the late nineteenth and early twentieth centuries.

Merton College, Oxford, one of university's oldest colleges. © Nicola Lisle

The Association for the Education of Women in Oxford, founded in 1878, paved the way for the opening of several women-only halls of residence. Lady Margaret Hall opened that same year, followed by St Anne's and Somerville (1879), St Hugh's (1886) and St Hilda's (1893).

Women were allowed to attend university lectures from 1880, and to sit exams from 1884, but they were not eligible for full membership of the university and the right to be awarded degrees until 1920. Even then the battle was not over; the number of female undergraduates was officially limited to a quarter that of male undergraduates until 1957, and women's colleges were not given full collegiate status until 1959.

All the constituent colleges of Oxford University remained single-sex until 1974, when Brasenose, Jesus, Wadham, Hertford and St

Catherine's became the first to open their doors to female undergraduates. Among the women-only colleges, St Anne's and Lady Margaret Hall were the first to admit men in 1979, followed by St Hugh's in 1986 and Somerville in 1994. St Hilda's was the last college to become mixed-sex, admitting men for the first time as recently as 2008.

THE STEAMBOAT LADIES

Between 1904 and 1907, female students from Oxford and Cambridge who had successfully completed the examinations required for a degree travelled by steamboat to Trinity College, Dublin, where they were awarded BA and MA degrees 'ad eundem'. Their method of transport earned them the nickname 'steamboat ladies'. It is estimated that around 700 steamboat ladies were awarded degrees by Trinity College during this three-year period.

Records for the steamboat ladies can be found in the indices to the Trinity College entrance books, which give each student's name, date of entry, name of tutor and whether they entered from Oxford or Cambridge. The college's *Catalogue of Graduates* gives the dates on which they obtained their degrees. For more information, visit www.tcd.ie/library/manuscripts/index.php

University records

Oxford University Archives

The Oxford University Archives holds administrative records for the university from 1214 onwards, and this includes records of students and academic staff. For students, this covers the three stages of life at the university: matriculation (i.e. the formal process of being admitted to the university), examinations and graduation. Archive staff provide a free research service, but it is useful to have an idea of the records they have available and what kind of information they contain.

Matriculation forms exist mainly from 1870 to 1932, and include the student's name, college, date and place of birth, home address and father's name and profession. These forms were handwritten by the student, which means they can be useful for comparing with other handwritten documents to confirm identity.

University admission is a two-stage process: students are admitted first to an individual college, which then presents them for admission to the university. This means that colleges also hold individual records, which are usually more detailed (see 'College Archives' on page 128).

Records before 1870 are somewhat sketchy, as the university didn't start keeping formal records until the late sixteenth century, and even then they were inconsistent. **Matriculation registers** and **subscription registers** were established in the early seventeenth century; the latter also contain signatures, as students had to subscribe to 'The Thirty-Nine Articles' of the Church of England on matriculation.

The **Undergraduate Process Register** began around 1880 and recorded details of all exams passed by each student. This will show you the academic progress of your ancestor and the principal subject studied. Note that single-subject degrees weren't introduced until the late nineteenth century. Most students would simply study for a BA, which covered a range of subjects including Latin, Greek, maths and philosophy. It was also common up to the early twentieth century for people to go to Oxford for a few terms, pass some exams and then leave without obtaining a degree.

For those that did obtain degrees, the **Degree Conferral records** confirm the subject passed, the kind of degree obtained (i.e. whether honours were conferred or not) and which college they attended.

Records for female undergraduates are sparse before 1920, but they were required to register, despite not being eligible for degrees, so some registration and examination records from the late nineteenth century do exist. From 1920 onwards, the records are the same as for male undergraduates. Some women who had passed exams at Oxford before 1920 returned at the beginning of Michaelmas term that year to matriculate so that they could have degrees conferred on them the next day. Approximately forty women collected their degrees in this way, including the author Dorothy L. Sayers.

Records of female undergraduates were also kept by the Association for the Education of Women in Oxford, and their official records are held by the Bodleian Library's Special Collections department (see below).

Graduate students are recorded slightly differently. The admissions procedure is the opposite to undergraduate students: they are admitted to the university first, and then to an individual college. There is a full set of individual files for graduate students, but they only go back to the early twentieth century, when postgraduate and research degrees were introduced, and access to many of these will be restricted by data protection.

Academic staff are recorded from the nineteenth century onwards, but again many later records will be restricted. Material may include correspondence about members of staff, as well as an academic file giving details such as date of appointment, date of resignation and reports on their work throughout the academic year.

It is worth noting that people in the nineteenth century and earlier were in the habit of exaggerating their links with Oxford University, so it is possible that your ancestor might appear to have been at Oxford only for this to turn out not to have been the case. According to Archives staff, only about 20 per cent of enquiries made to them yield positive results.

There are further resources on open shelves in the Bodleian's Duke Humfrey Reading Room, but you will need to apply for a Reader's Ticket to view them (See Chapter 1).

Useful publications relating to the matriculation and subscription registers are A.B. Emden's *A Biographical Register of the University of Oxford to AD1500* (3 vols, 1957) and *A Biographical Register of the University of Oxford AD1501 to 1540* (1 vol, 1974); and Joseph Foster's *Alumni Oxonienses 1500–1714* (2 vols, 1891–2), *Alumni Oxonienses*

1715–1886 (2 vols, 1891–2), and *Oxford Men and their Colleges* (2 vols, 1893). These are the most detailed compilations available, with information drawn from the University Archives records and a variety of other sources.

Digitised copies of Foster's books are available on the Internet Archive website, www.bodleian.ox.ac.uk/oua/enquiries/members-guide.

Other useful sources include the *University Calendar*, which has been produced annually since 1810 and includes details of degrees obtained in a specific year, and the *Examination Statutes*, which give details of past examination papers so you can see what kind of exams your ancestor might have taken. There is also a full set of the *University Gazette*, which dates from 1870 and has all kinds of useful information that can help give clues about life at the university for your ancestor.

Bodleian Library Special Collections

This is where you can delve a little deeper in your ancestor's university life, but again you will need a Reader's Ticket to gain access (see above). Principal holdings here include personal papers, collections relating to official university organisations and records of student clubs and societies.

A useful starting point is to consult the various guides to the collections, as these give detailed information about what's available and where it can be found. One of the most comprehensive is *A Bibliography of Printed Works Relating to the University of Oxford* (E.H. Cordeaux and D.H. Merry, Clarendon Press, 1968, ref. 213). This covers material relating to the history of the university, including examinations, degrees, diplomas, certificates, scholarships, prizes, faculties, clubs and societies, individual colleges and associated institutions.

The *Summary Catalogue of Post-Medieval Western Manuscripts in the Bodleian Library Oxford – Acquisitions 1916–75* (Mary Clapinson and T.D. Rogers, Clarendon Press, 1991, ref. 705/3) lists individuals alphabetically and gives their dates of birth and death as well as all correspondence and other papers relating to them.

A similar publication is *Summary Catalogue of Manuscripts in the Bodleian Library Accessions 1916–1962* (P.S. Spokes, Bodleian Library, 1964, ref. 704). The general index is particularly useful, as you can look up individuals or clubs and societies and get details of related letters, books, poems, maps, paintings, surveys and more.

Finally, *The Bodleian Library: A Subject Guide to the Collections* (edited by Geoffrey Walker, Mary Clapinson and Lesley Forbes, Bodleian Library, 2004, ref. 200), gives a detailed outline of the library's resources.

If your university ancestor was a freemason, he was probably a member of the **Apollo University Lodge**, which was formed in 1818. Distinguished former members include Cecil Rhodes, Oscar Wilde, Prince Leopold and Prince Albert Edward (later King Edward VII). Papers relating to the Lodge include accounts 1880–1996, membership records 1818–1993, minutes of meetings 1818–2002 and miscellaneous papers 1824–2005. Access is subject to a closure of fifty years. The material is catalogued, with shelf marks indicated. The catalogue is also available online.

Papers for the **Association for the Education of Women in Oxford** (AEW) from 1878–1922 include minute books, financial records, correspondence, lecture lists, annual reports, calendars and other miscellaneous papers. Records relating specifically to students include a general register of students 1891–1920, with details of terms attended and exams taken; a special register of BA students 1894–1913; a register of foreign students 1908–14; records of students' residencies; a records of assignment of students to tutors, arranged by subject within each term for 1907–20 and by college within each term for 1912–20; and notebooks of teaching given to students, arranged by institution 1883–1901, with some student reports.

There are also minutes of meetings held for the committee organising 'Lectures for Ladies', the forerunner of the AEW, 1873–76.

Again, these papers are catalogued, with shelf marks indicated. You can also access this online: http://www.bodley.ox.ac.uk/dept/scwmss/wmss/online/modern/aew/aew.html.

Records for the various student clubs and societies are patchy, sadly, largely because of the transient nature of their memberships. Record-keeping was entirely down to the efficiency or otherwise of the club or society officers from one university year to another. The collections are worth a look, though, especially if you know your ancestor was definitely involved in one of the university clubs or societies, as you might be lucky enough to find something – even if it simply confirms your ancestor's membership and relevant dates.

Exceptions are the **Oxford University Boat Club**, for which you will find newsletters from 1945–91, and the **Oxford University Dramatic Society (OUDS)**, which has retained minute books, correspondence, accounts and other miscellaneous papers covering 1932–57.

Material relating to clubs and societies can also be found within the **John Johnson Collection** (www.bodleian.ox.ac.uk/johnson/about), one of the largest collections of printed ephemera in the world. The collection was started in the 1930s by John Johnson, a papyrologist and later Printer to the University of Oxford, and comprises what Johnson himself called 'a little museum of common printed things'. Among the million and a half items are playbills and programmes for concerts and theatre productions. Originally housed at the OUP, the collection was deposited with the Bodleian in 1968 and is in the process of being digitised. You can search the catalogues at www.bodleian.ox.ac.uk/johnson/search/catalogue/online-catalogue. An exhibition of Johnson's collection was held at the Bodleian Library in 1971, and the exhibition catalogue, *John Johnson Collection: Catalogue of an Exhibition* (shelf mark 361) gives a good overview of the kind of material it includes.

It is also worth looking through old college and university in-house magazines such as *Isis*, which has a section called 'Oxford Idols' that gives details of student achievements. These magazines are held off-site at the University's storage facility in Swindon, so you need to request them so that they can be brought in.

College archives

All the constituent colleges of Oxford University have their own archives, and these vary from one college to another. Most, though, will typically hold their own administrative records and correspondence relating to former members, as well as personal papers, estate records and other archival material. In additional to personal details and academic progress, undergraduate records may include sporting achievements, clubs or societies belonged to and so on, all helping to build up a broader picture of your ancestor's extra-curricular skills and interests. You can easily find details of college archives and how to contact their archivists on the individual college websites.

SCHOOLS

Early education in Oxfordshire came largely from grammar schools and charity schools, as well as from the three Oxford choral foundations at New College School (founded by William Wykeham, the Bishop of Winchester, in 1379), Magdalen College School (founded by William Waynflete in 1480) and Christ Church Cathedral Schools (founded by Henry VIII in 1546). One of the longest-running charity schools was Nixon's School in Oxford, which was founded in 1658 for the sons of freemen and was demolished in the late nineteenth century to make way for the new Town Hall.

Other charity schools – known as Blue Coat, Green Coat or Grey Coat schools – were established for children of labourers and prepared them for apprenticeships in local industries. The Blue Coat School in Witney, for example, was set up in 1723 by cloth merchant John Holloway, who financed twelve scholarships for the sons of local weavers. By 1833 the school was taking fee-paying pupils as well, and the scholarship pupils were distinguishable by their blue coats.

Parochial schools were established from the late seventeenth century as part of a UK-wide initiative by the Society for Promoting Christian Knowledge (SPCK) to provide education for the poor. The Declaration of Indulgence in 1672 and the Toleration Act of 1689 allowed non-conformist religions to set up their own day schools. John Wesley established a school in St Ebbe's, Oxford, in 1726, but the first Baptist and Roman Catholic schools didn't appear in the city until the early nineteenth century.

Oxfordshire's Church of England primary schools have their origins in the National Schools set up by the National Society for the Promotion of Education, which was founded in 1811 to provide education for the poor. From 1839 they were supported in this mission by the Oxford Diocesan Board of Education. School Boards came into existence after the Elementary Education Act of 1870, and Board Schools were established in parishes where they were most needed. Education became compulsory from 1880.

Major educational reform came in 1902 with the Education Act, which introduced the provision of state-funded schools for all children aged five to thirteen. Many of the earlier religious schools were gradually absorbed into the new system. The school leaving age was raised to fifteen by the 1944 Education Act, and to sixteen in 1972.

School records

Survival of early school records is poor; most of those held by the OHC date from the late nineteenth and early twentieth centuries, and can be found in the parish and borough collections. For example, the school attendance officer's reports for Chipping Norton Schools for 1878–91 can be found in the Chipping Norton Borough Records catalogue (BOR1/2/A2). These include the officer's attendance return, attendance report and report on absentee children.

Admission registers, if they exist, are the most useful, as they include pupils' names, addresses and dates of birth. School log books can also be helpful for giving an idea of what life was like at a particular school. Sadly, there was no requirement for schools to keep records, so many of these have not survived. Records for schools that still exist are likely to have been retained by the school, so if you know which school your ancestor went to it is best to contact the school direct.

The OHC's main holding for schools is the Macclesfield House School Records collection (CC4), which resulted from a survey of all county council-run schools during the early 1900s and consists largely of records concerning the structural condition of each school, the equipment and staffing provided, heating and lighting, sanitary arrangements, size of pupil rolls, medical officers' reports, out of hours activities, accounts, records of charitable bequests, ground plans and photographs. Many of the plans and photographs have been digitised and can be searched on Picture Oxon (http://pictureoxon.com). The collection covers nearly 250 Oxfordshire schools.

There are also records relating to schools and relevant individuals in the Business Index and in local newspapers, as well as recordings in the oral history collection.

ADULT EDUCATION

From the 1820s, mechanics' institutes started to appear in towns and cities across the UK to provide technical education for working-class adults. They were often founded by philanthropists to improve life for the poor. For example, a mechanics' institute was set up in Banbury in 1835 and provided a library as well as regular lectures and exhibitions. In 1884, local industrialist Sir Bernhard Samuelson paid for the relocation of the institute to larger premises in Marlborough Road, in the building now used as the local library. This led to the foundation of the Banbury School of Arts and Sciences. The OHC holds records of the Banbury Mechanics' Institute (series O51); the collection includes committee and sub-committee minutes, accounts, manuscript magazines, plans and photographs.

In Oxford, there were several institutes and schools providing day and evening classes in science and arts throughout much of the nineteenth century, with many gradually expanding to cater for both adults and under eighteens.

The Oxford School of Art, established in 1865, went through several mergers and changes of name to become, in 1934, the Schools of Technology, Art and Commerce, offering full-time undergraduate courses as well as evening classes for adults. The school's first principal, John Henry Brookes, was a major influence in the development of the institution, which by the 1950s was spread over nineteen sites across the city. Brookes campaigned to bring all departments onto one campus, and in 1955 the schools moved to Headington, changing the name again a year later to the Oxford College of Technology. In 1970 the college became Oxford Polytechnic, coming under Oxfordshire County Council control four years later. The Oxford School of Nursing was incorporated in 1988, and in 1992, following new government legislation, Oxford Polytechnic became Oxford Brookes University.

John Henry Brookes was honoured with a blue plaque in 2011. © Nicola Lisle

The Oxford Brookes University Collection (www.brookes.ac.uk/library/special-collections/oxford-brookes-university/oxford-brookes-university-collection) has papers relating to the history of the university, including principals' reports, committee minutes, publicity material, press cuttings, staff and student magazines and prospectuses, as well as papers relating to John Henry Brookes.

The OHC also has some records relating to Oxford Brookes and its predecessors; use Heritage Search to find what you are looking for. Local newspapers often carry news about colleges and adult education institutions, including changes of name and location, and obituaries of staff and former students. The oral history and photographic collections also have relevant material.

The Archives Hub (www.archiveshub.ac.uk) has details of various archives and manuscript collections for adult education institutions and colleges of higher education.

The *Victoria County History* has a detailed history of City of Oxford schools and adult education at www.british-history.ac.uk/vch/oxon/vol4/pp442-462. The Oxfordshire History website has a section on Oxford schools in the late nineteenth and early twentieth centuries, including lists of schools, at www.oxfordhistory.org.uk/schools/index.html.

FURTHER READING

Oxford University

Adams, Pauline, *Somerville for Women: An Oxford College 1879–1993*, OUP, 1996

Brittain, Vera, *The Women at Oxford: A Fragment of History*, Harrap, 1960

Brockliss, L.W.B., *The University of Oxford: A History*, OUP, 2016

Evans, G.R., *The University of Oxford: A New History*, Touris, 2013

Jenkinson, Matthew, *New College School, Oxford: A History*, Shire Publications, 2013

Bodleian Library

Clapinson, Mary, *A Brief History of the Bodleian Library*, The Bodleian Library, 2015

Clapinson, Mary and Rogers, T.D., *Summary Catalogue of Post-*

Medieval Western Manuscripts in the Bodleian Library Oxford – Acquisitions 1916–75, Clarendon Press, 1991

Cock-Starkey, Claire, *Bodleianalia: Curious Facts About Britain's Oldest University Library*, The Bodleian Library, 2016

Cordeaux, E.H. and Merry, D.H., *A Bibliography of Printed Works Relating to the University of Oxford*, Clarendon Press, 1968

Spokes, P.S., *Summary Catalogue of Manuscripts in the Bodleian Library Accessions 1916–1962*, Bodleian Library, 1964

Walker, Geoffrey, Clapinson, Mary and Forbes, Lesley (eds), *The Bodleian Library: A Subject Guide to the Collections*, Bodleian Library, 2004

Other

Brown, Bryan, *John Henry Brookes: The Man Who Inspired a University*, Oxford Brookes University, 2015

Chapter 8

OXFORDSHIRE AT WAR

OXFORDSHIRE REGIMENTS

The Oxfordshire Yeomanry

Oxfordshire's oldest regiment was formed in 1794 as a volunteer defence force to help counteract civil unrest and the threat of invasion by Napoleon's troops. Responding to a call by the Lord Lieutenant, the 4th Duke of Marlborough, the volunteers were drawn largely from the nobility and landed classes, hence the name. For the next hundred or so years, the Oxfordshire Yeomanry played an important role in keeping the peace, and later saw action in the Boer War and both world wars.

The first unit was the Oxfordshire Fencible Troop, which was based at Watlington and raised by the Earl of Macclesfield in 1798. Further units followed, and eventually most of these were amalgamated to form the First Regiment of the Oxfordshire Yeomanry Cavalry under the command of Francis Almeric Spencer, the first Lord Churchill and brother of the 5th Duke of Marlborough.

In 1835, Queen Adelaide, wife of William IV, granted the Oxfordshire Yeomanry the right to use the title 'The Queen's Own' in their name after they provided an escort during her visit to Oxford. The *Oxford Jackson's Journal* described how the Queen's cavalcade 'was escorted by two small bodies of Lord Churchill's Regiment of Oxfordshire Cavalry and swept forward at a most rapid pace'. The royal recognition led to the change of name to the Queen's Own Oxfordshire Hussars (QOOH).

The outbreak of the Boer War in 1899 saw the establishment of the Imperial Yeomanry, with the Duke of Marlborough and Viscount Valentia, CO of the QOOH, involved in organising this new force. Around 20,000 men from the Yeomanry regiments across England answered the call for volunteers, including 250 from Oxfordshire. For many it was their first taste of real warfare, and inevitably some never returned.

A blue plaque marks the spot in Cornmarket, Oxford, where the Oxfordshire Yeomanry first gathered in 1794. © Nicola Lisle

In August 1914, the QOOH became the first territorial unit to see action in the First World War when they were attached to Winston Churchill's Naval Brigade, taking part in campaigns at Flanders, Ypres and Amiens. For much of this time they were fighting alongside regular troops in the trenches.

After the war the QOOH became an artillery unit, and by the outbreak of the Second World War had become the 63rd (Oxfordshire Yeomanry) Anti-Tank Regiment, serving on the home front in England and Ireland before being despatched to France in October 1944, on Churchill's orders. Some of the regiment served in Singapore, where they found themselves among the 60,000 prisoners forced to work on the notorious Burma Railway, while others were among the first Allied troops to go into Belsen.

After the Second World War the QOOH underwent a number of reincarnations, including amalgamation with the Royal Bucks Yeomanry in 1947 and the Berkshire Yeomanry in 1956. Defence cuts forced the disbanding of the QOOH in 1967, but they re-formed in 1971 as a Royal Signals unit based in Banbury. More recently, they became part of the Royal Logistics Corps.

The Star Inn in Oxford, where the volunteers first gathered in 1794, has long since been demolished, but the site was marked with a blue plaque in 2003.

QOOH AND THE CHURCHILL CONNECTION

Winston Leonard Spencer Churchill was born in 1874 at Blenheim Palace, Woodstock, the seat of the dukes of Marlborough. After a short military career with the Fourth Hussars, serving in Cuba, India and Sudan, he became the Conservative MP for Oldham, Lancashire, in 1900, aged twenty-six. He joined the Woodstock Squadron of the Queen's Own Oxfordshire Hussars as captain in January 1902, and was promoted to major in April 1905 and appointed to command the Henley Squadron.

It was Churchill's influence that led to the QOOH's involvement in both world wars. In September 1914, the QOOH became the first territorial regiment to join the regular troops when Churchill, as First Lord of the Admiralty, ordered their embarkation to France to support the Naval Division. He became Honorary Colonel in 1927, retaining this title until his death in January 1965.

Controversially, he left sealed instructions that the QOOH should march ahead of his coffin at his state funeral procession in London, an honour that would normally have gone to one of the more senior regiments. He was buried in the family plot at St Martin's Church, Bladon, just outside Woodstock.

Oxfordshire and Buckinghamshire Light Infantry

Oxfordshire's other main regiment is the Oxfordshire and Buckinghamshire Light Infantry, which was officially formed on 1 July 1881 from the amalgamation of the 43rd (Monmouthshire) Regiment of Foot (Light Infantry) and the 52nd (Oxfordshire) Regiment of Foot (Light Infantry). Both regiments already had long and distinguished histories: the 43rd was raised in 1741 as Colonel Fowke's Regiment of Foot, and the 52nd in 1755 as the 54th Regiment of Foot, being renumbered two years later. The latter was based at Cowley Barracks in Oxford, and saw action during the American War of Independence (1775–78) and the French Revolutionary Wars (1793–1801).

The 43rd and 52nd were both redesignated as Light Infantry regiments in 1803, and fought in the Peninsular War (1808–14) and the Indian Mutiny (1857–58). The 52nd also fought in the Battle of Waterloo in 1815.

The amalgamation of the two regiments was part of the reformation of the infantry regiments by Hugh Childers, the Secretary of State for War. Initially known as the Oxfordshire Light Infantry, in 1908 it was renamed the Oxfordshire and Buckinghamshire Light Infantry. The new amalgamated regiment saw action during both world wars, winning numerous battle honours and individual gallantry medals. Two members of the Oxfordshire and Buckinghamshire Light Infantry were awarded Victoria Crosses for their actions during the First World War: Headington resident Company Sergeant Major Edward Brooks, and Birmingham-born Lance-Corporal Alfred Wilcox, both of the 2/4th battalion. You can read Brooks' citation in the *London Gazette* at www.thegazette.co.uk/London/issue/30154/supplement/6381, and Wilcox's at www.thegazette.co.uk/London/issue/31012/supplement/ 13473.

In 1958 the regiment joined the Green Jackets Brigade, and on 1 January 1966 merged with the King's Royal Rifle Corps and the Rifle Brigade to form the Royal Green Jackets.

The official Oxfordshire and Buckinghamshire Light Infantry war memorial was unveiled at Rose Hill, Oxford, in 1923. The Grade II listed memorial was designed by Sir Edwin Lutyens.

The Oxford University Officer Training Corps

The OUOTC came into being in 1908 following the creation of the Officers' Training Corps (OTC) by Richard Haldane, Secretary of State for War, as a way of encouraging young men to enrol in the regular army. An existing Oxford University Rifle Volunteer Corps, formed in 1859, was incorporated into the OUOTC, which was based at the University Delegacy for Military Instruction in Albert Street, Oxford. Officers from the regular army trained the cadets during term time.

After the outbreak of the First World War, a School of Instruction was established for trainee officers, and this evolved into two Officer Cadet Battalions, No.4 Oxford and No.6 Balliol College, in 1916. Around 2,000 members of the OUOTC lost their lives during the conflict. The end of the Second World War saw the Senior Divisions of the OUOTC absorbed into the Territorial Army. Women were admitted to the OUOTC for the first time in 1948, but trained separately from the men until the 1960s. The Corps is currently based in Oxpens Road, Oxford, following several changes of headquarters during the twentieth century.

MILITARY RESOURCES

There are millions of military documents available online and in various local and national archives, so there is a good chance of being able to find records relating to your military ancestor. It will save a lot of time if you know which service your ancestor was in, along with other details such as rank, regiment/ship/unit and dates of service.

Local resources

The Soldiers of Oxfordshire Trust Museum and Archive

Established in 2014 from the amalgamation of the Trustees of the Oxfordshire and Buckinghamshire Light Infantry, the Trustees of the

The Soldiers of Oxfordshire Museum in Woodstock. © Nicola Lisle

Oxfordshire Yeomanry and the Soldiers of Oxfordshire Trust, this is the main archive for the Oxfordshire regiments. The collections date from the eighteenth century and cover the regiments' involvement in the two world wars as well as earlier conflicts. SOFO holds well over 120,000 records for soldiers and officers who served with the Oxfordshire regiments from 1899 onwards. Holdings also include documents relating to the Oxford University Officers Training Corps. Visits to the library and archive are by appointment; alternatively, research can be undertaken by volunteers, for which a fee is payable. Check that your ancestor is in the archive through the Soldier Search facility (www.sofo.org.uk/soldiers/soldier) and then contact the archive in writing or via their online enquiry form (www.sofo.org.uk/archive-enquiry). A basic enquiry (for £50) will include your ancestor's full name, date and place of birth, serial number, battalion, date of discharge and/or death, medals awarded and service record summary.

You can also explore SOFO's holdings through the OHC's Heritage Search. If you find items of interest, contact SOFO quoting the reference numbers.

Some of SOFO's holdings for the Oxfordshire and Buckinghamshire Light Infantry are on loan from the Royal Green Jacket (Rifles) Museum in Winchester (http://rgjmuseum.co.uk), which also has displays relating to the history of the regiment.

Oxford History Centre

Although the main archive for the Oxfordshire regiments is with SOFO, the OHC has a large collection of papers relating to the two world wars. The papers of the Oxford Territorial Army Association and the local Home Guard can be found in series O11/1 and O11/2 respectively, and include minutes of meetings, central government circulars, correspondence, lists of members and photographs. Series O144 relates to the Oxford Fire Fighters and Watchers' Corps, which was established in 1941 by local businesses to protect their properties from incendiary attacks.

There are also papers relating to local RAF bases including site plans, former RAF schools, closure of former air bases, minute books and personal papers. Series P441, for example, contains the war records of Morris Motors carpenter Edward Mobley, who spent the Second World War working for 50 M.U., an RAF maintenance unit based at Cowley Barracks and responsible for recovering damaged aircraft all over the country. The series includes his account of his experiences, additional notes by his son and a collection of photographs.

Search the OHC's newspaper collection for war-related news, lists of local casualties and gallantry awards, obituaries of local servicemen, and other relevant features. The Photographic and Oral History collections have hundreds of items relating mainly to the Second World War – search or browse the collections at Picture Oxon (http://pictureoxon.com/).

Finally, individual employers and institutions often had their own records of members of staff who served in the two world wars. If you know which organisation your ancestor worked for, use Heritage Search to find relevant records. Alternatively, contact organisations direct – for example, Oxford University Press (see Chapter 6) and the Bodleian Library for university records (see Chapter 7).

Oxford University Archives

The OUA at the Bodleian Library (www.bodliean.ox.ac.uk/oua/holdings/catalogues) has more information about the history of the OUOTC as well as an extensive archive of documents including appointment letters, service records, lists of officers and cadets, enrolment registers, nominations for commissions into the regular army, details of military training, publicity materials, photographs and financial and administrative papers. The website has a downloadable PDF giving a detailed list of the archive's holdings (scroll down the page to 'Records of University departments').

The *Oxford University Roll of Service*, edited by E.S. Craig and W.M. Gibson (Clarendon Press, 1920) has been digitised and can be browsed or searched at https://archive.org/details/oxforduniversity00univuoft.

National Resources

The National Archives

The TNA is the principal repository for service records and other papers relating to all branches of the armed forces. Search the Discovery catalogue (http://discovery.nationalarchives.gov.uk) for TNA's own holdings as well as records from other archives across the UK. The TNA research guide to military and maritime records (www.nationalarchives.gov.uk/help-with-your-research/research-guides/?research-category=military-and-maritime) gives a good overview and includes links to other research guides and resources, including those for the Army, Royal Navy, Merchant Navy and Royal Air Force (including its predecessors, the Royal Flying Corps and the

Royal Naval Air Service). Holdings include service and pension records, discharge documents, medal index cards and rolls, casualty lists, muster rolls, recommendations for honours and awards, courts martial and desertion, war diaries, ships' logs and journals, crew lists, operation books and Prisoner of War records. A large number of these records are available to view online; some can be downloaded free of charge (tagged Digital Microfilm), while for others a fee is payable. There are many more records that can only be viewed in the TNA searchroom. The TNA website redirects to Findmypast for British Army casualty lists for the Second World War (https://search.findmypast.co.uk/search-world-records/british-army-casualty-lists-1939-1945) and to Ancestry for First World War soldiers' service and pension records (https://search.ancestry.co.uk/search/category.aspx?cat=39). Both websites hold many more records relating to military service.

Museum Archives

The National Army Museum (www.nam.ac.uk) has an extensive archive and library as well as five galleries of themed displays relating to the history of the British Army. Search the online object and book inventories by key words such as name, regiment or unit, war, battle, campaign or place for a list of relevant items in the museum's collections together with their location and accession number. The Templer Study Centre (www.nam.ac.uk/collections/templer-study-centre) has over 55,000 books on British military history, plus large collections of maps, photographs and archival material, and is particularly good for regimental and campaign histories. You will need a reader's card, which is free and can be obtained on the day you visit upon production of two forms of identity.

Find other army museums and archives related to your ancestor's regiment through the Army Museums Ogilby Trust (www.armymuseums.org.uk); search by regiment, collection or region. The website also has advice on tracing military ancestors, with useful links, and runs regular training courses and events.

For naval ancestors, the National Museum of the Royal Navy (www.royalnavy.mod.uk) provides links to various ships and museums in its care, including HMS *Victory* and the Royal Navy in Portsmouth, the Fleet Air Arm Museum at Yeovilton and many more. All have important collections and archives relating to different aspects of the history of the Royal Navy.

Similarly, the Royal Air Force Museum (www.rafmuseum.org.uk) has collections at Hendon and Cosford relating to the history of the RAF since its formation in 1918. The reading room at Hendon is open by appointment. The archive includes personal papers (letters, memoirs and diaries), aircrew logbooks, aircraft accidents, First World War casualty cards, books and periodicals and ephemera. The Research page has several downloadable research guides to get you started.

Useful Websites

The Wartime Memories Project (www.wartimememoriesproject.com) has detailed regimental histories for both world wars, with both of the Oxfordshire regiments included. As well as battle and campaign information, the website also includes lists of men known to have served with each regiment. An online library of records, personal papers and photographs is available by subscription only.

Forces War Records (www.forces-war-records.co.uk) has exclusive transcriptions of selected casualty rolls, war lists, auxiliary units, officer lists, Prisoners of War lists, military hospital admission and discharge registers, rolls of honour, medal rolls and army lists, as well as other transcriptions, records from other archives and original records. Their online journal includes historical features and genealogy guides, and is well worth a read. You need to create a free account to get access to all parts of the website.

The *London Gazette* (www.thegazette.co.uk), the official government newspaper launched in 1665, carries notices of service appointments, promotions, awards and deaths, and can be searched online. For example, a search for Sergeant Edward John Mott, who

Exterior of the Imperial War Museum in London, containing the Lord Ashcroft Gallery. © *Nicola Lisle*

was born in Drayton, near Abingdon, and served with the Border Regiment, brings up the citation for his Victoria Cross, which he was awarded in March 1917 for 'most conspicuous gallantry and initiative' while under machine-gun fire in France. The website includes advice on how to get the most out of your searches.

Lord Ashcroft has built up the world's largest collection of Victoria Crosses, which are now on display in the Lord Ashcroft Gallery at the Imperial War Museum in London. Details of the Victoria Crosses are on Lord Ashcroft's Medal Collection website (www.lord ashcroftmedals.com), listed by surname, conflict, year gazetted and service.

WAR GRAVES AND MEMORIALS

War memorials became commonplace in the UK in the aftermath of the First World War, and they reflect both the sheer scale of the devastation and the overwhelming sense of loss felt by people at the time. The need to honour the war dead was even greater if there was no known grave. As well as providing an emotional connection to your ancestors, war graves and memorials can also be useful for confirming biographical details.

The Commonwealth War Graves Commission (www.cwgc.org) is the largest database of graves and memorials relating to servicemen who died in the two world wars. You can search the site by person or cemetery. Each personal record gives the full name, date of death, age at death, location of cemetery and any memorials, regiment and country of service. A search for Oxford's double VC-recipient Captain Noel Chavasse, for example, shows that he died on Saturday 4 August 1917, aged thirty-two, was buried at Brandhoek New Military Cemetery in Belgium and served with the Royal Army Medical Corps. Family details are also included, along with the inscription on his gravestone and transcriptions of his two VC citations. A commemorative certificate is available to download as a PDF – a particularly nice keepsake for any family historian.

A search for Oxfordshire war cemeteries shows that there are 170 scattered across the county. The largest is Oxford (Botley) Cemetery, which has the graves of more than 700 casualties of the two world wars. Click to see the list of all those buried there; each person listed has a link to their biographical details.

Oxfordshire also has around 100 free-standing memorials, as well as memorial plaques and tablets, memorial windows, rolls of honour and many more. The majority commemorate those who died during the two world wars, and range from simple columns or plaques to more elaborate designs. The war memorial at Chipping Norton, for example, takes the form of a large stone wall fronted by smaller walls and steps, with a central memorial plaque flanked by separate tablets listing those who died in each of the two world wars. On one of the outer walls is a blue plaque honouring General Sir Montagu Stopford, who lived nearby and served with distinction in both wars.

War Memorial at Chipping Norton. © Nicola Lisle

Many of Oxford University's colleges have their own memorials to staff and students who fought in the two world wars. Noel Chavasse, for example, is included on the Roll of Honour in St Peter's College chapel, along with his younger brother, Aidan, who was also killed in action in 1917. The chapel includes a Chavasse memorial window and memorial tablets to other members of the Chavasse family, including Noel's father, Francis, who founded the college in 1929.

Some war memorials commemorate the fallen in earlier campaigns. One of the oldest is the Tirah Memorial in Bonn Square, Oxford, which was unveiled in 1900 to honour the soldiers of the 2nd Battalion Oxfordshire Light Infantry who lost their lives on the Tirah Expedition of 1897–98. Privates are listed by name only; for other ranks, the cause of death is included.

Roll of Honour at St Peter's College Chapel, with the names of Noel and Aidan Chavasse. *© Nicola Lisle*

Altar and Chavasse window, St Peter's College Chapel. *© Nicola Lisle*

Oxford's most recent memorial, unveiled in St Clement's in June 2017 after a three-year campaign, is the Spanish Civil War memorial, which commemorates the thirty-one Oxfordshire men and women who fought against General Franco's army from 1936–39. Six were killed in action.

The SOFO website has a list of Oxfordshire war memorials (www.sofo.org.uk/oxfordshires-war-memorials), arranged alphabetically by place. The OHC has records of the various War Memorial Committees set up in parishes across Oxfordshire, and these include original drawings and other details relating to the design of the memorials. Search the Parish Councils collections, or use Heritage Search to find the memorial relevant to your ancestor.

You can also search the Imperial War Museum's national War Memorials Register at www.iwm.org.uk/corporate/projects-and-partnerships/war-memorials-register. This has details of more than a thousand Oxfordshire war memorials.

The Oxfordshire page of the Roll of Honour website (www.roll-of-honour.com/Oxfordshire) is a fantastic resource. This is part of an ongoing project to transcribe all war memorials and rolls of honour in the UK, and there is already a vast amount of information available. Search by place name to see a picture and description of its war memorial and/or roll of honour, together with a list of those commemorated and their biographies. Details include full name, rank, regiment, date and place of death, age at death, parents' names, previous regiments, location of grave (if known) and any other memorials. Note that the site is arranged geographically by the pre-1974 county boundaries, so you may need to search the Berkshire and Buckinghamshire pages as well.

Another ongoing project is the Oxfordshire and Buckinghamshire Light Infantry Roll of Honour (http://oxfordandbucks.co.uk/Roll_of_Honour.htm). Details include service number, rank, full name, company, where enlisted, date and cause of death, age at death and location of grave and/or memorial. The site also has transcripts of war diaries, a photo gallery and trench maps.

The Banbury War Memorial site (www.sjbradley.com/memorial) includes a list of all Banbury men who died during the Second World War. Biographies are similar to those on the Oxfordshire Roll of Honour site, but also include mother's maiden name and parents' date of marriage.

The Oxford History site (www.oxfordhistory.org.uk/war/index.html) has a list of Oxford war memorials, again with pictures, descriptions and biographies, plus some useful links.

LIFE ON THE HOME FRONT

The First World War brought unprecedented changes to the British way of life. Conscription and food rationing were introduced in Britain for the first time, and women had to take on jobs traditionally regarded as 'men's work', such as driving buses and taxis, working in factories and becoming ticket inspectors or car mechanics. On top of this, there was the constant fear of air raids, the gradual loss of shops and businesses as staff were called away to fight, the introduction of fuel and lighting restrictions and many other hardships.

Despite this, people threw themselves wholeheartedly into supporting the war effort, raising vital funds, carrying out voluntary work and providing entertainments and comforts for the troops. People also volunteered for civil defence organisations, including the Home Guard and Air Raid Precautions.

Numerous buildings in Oxfordshire were converted for military purposes. The Third Southern General Hospital, launched in Oxford in August 1914, took over university and public buildings including the Town Hall, the Oxford Examination Schools, Oxford Eye Hospital, Radcliffe Infirmary, Wingfield Convalescent Home in Headington and many more. The Oxford Orthopaedic Hospital was set up in the Wingfield's grounds and still exists as the Nuffield Orthopaedic Centre. You can see details of buildings converted into hospitals during the First World War at www.oxfordshistory.org.uk/war/military_hospitals/index.html.

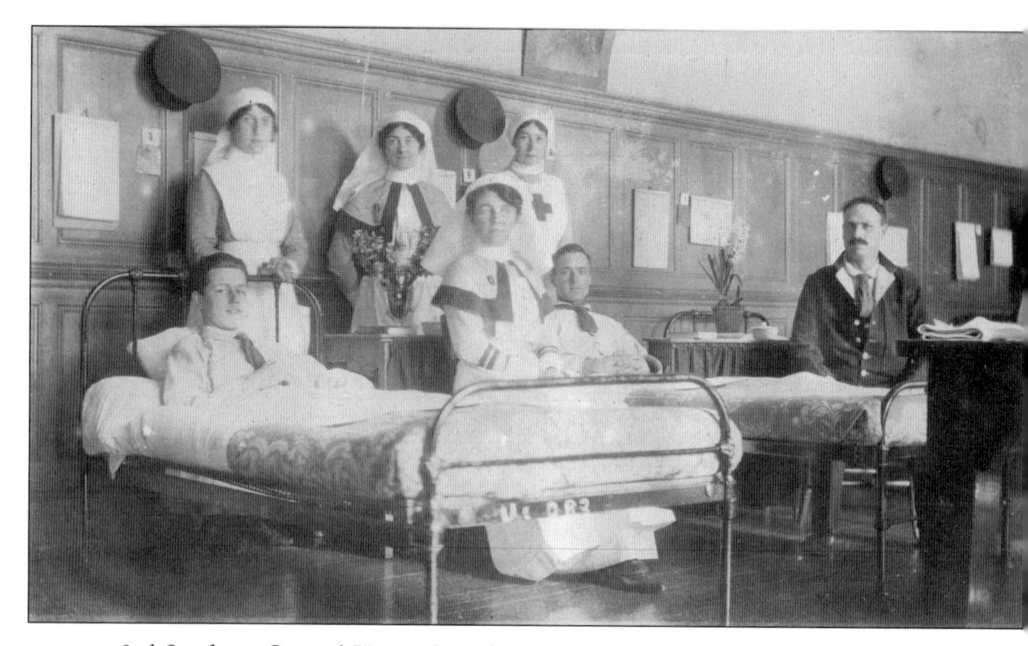

3rd Southern General Hospital, Oxford Section, WW1, © Oxfordshire County Council, Oxfordshire History Centre, Ref. D267999a

During the Second World War, Blenheim Palace in Woodstock was pressed into service as a home for boys evacuated from Malvern College in Worcester. It was later taken over by the War Office, as was Cornbury Park in Charlbury.

The OHC has numerous records relating to civil defence, wartime committees and other volunteer organisations; see their guide at www.oxfordshire.gov.uk/cms/content/world-wars-1-and-2-sources.

Registration and conscription

In July 1915, as part of a military recruitment drive, the National Registration Act came into force, requiring everyone aged fifteen to sixty-five to register their details on 15 August. This enabled the authorities to identify how many male civilians might be eligible for war work or military service. When that failed to produce sufficient extra troops, the Military Service Act was passed in January 1916, introducing conscription for all single men between the ages of eighteen and forty-one, with the exception of clergymen, teachers and various other occupations. People could also be exempted on medical grounds. Conscription was extended to married men just four months later.

Not everyone was happy about being conscripted into the armed forces, and some objected on moral or religious grounds. Requests for exemptions were considered by local tribunals, not only for conscientious objectors but also for those with medical or occupational reasons. Most local tribunal papers were destroyed after the war, but the OHC holds some surviving records for the Banbury and Witney boroughs and for Oxford City. These can be traced through Heritage Search. TNA also has some information about conscientious objectors in both world wars at www.nationalarchives.gov.uk/help-with-your-research/research-guides/conscientious-objectors/.

The 1939 Register

The outbreak of the Second World War saw the introduction of the 1939 Register, established by the National Registration Act 1939, and this was far more comprehensive than the 1915 register. The details of more than 40 million people in England and Wales were recorded on 29th June 1939, and these were used to issue identity cards and ration books, track people's movements, maintain population statistics and control manpower. Entries are listed by address and include full name, gender, date of birth, marital status and occupation.

With the destruction of the 1931 census for England and Wales in an air raid, and in the absence of a 1941 census, the 1939 Register bridges a gap of 37 years and is a valuable resource for family historians. Note that records have been redacted for anyone born less than 100 years ago, unless you can provide proof that they have died. The register was originally digitised as a joint project by TNA and Findmypast.

TNA's very helpful guide to the register is at www.nationalarchives.gov.uk/help-with-your-research/research-guides/1939-register, and you can search the records free at www.findmypast.co.uk/

1939register, which also gives useful advice and background information.

In 2018 the register was added to Ancestry's collections, with the additional benefit of including details of whether people were in hospitals, asylum or prisons on the night of registration, indicated by the letters O (Officer), V (Visitor), S (Servant), P (Patient) and I (Inmate).

The register has also recently been added by MyHeritage (www.myheritage.com) but without the images.

Evacuees

Oxfordshire was designated a reception centre for evacuees from London early in 1939. In addition to official evacuees, it is estimated that there were thousands of unofficial evacuees who stayed with friends or relatives. One famous refugee from the London Blitz was the Chinese travel writer Chiang Yee, whose wartime stay in Oxford resulted in *The Silent Traveller in Oxford*, published in 1944.

The OHC holds extensive records relating to evacuees, including evacuee lists and registers, return of evacuees to London, examination forms, details of schools set up for evacuees, details of householders accommodating the evacuees and more. Most records are archived by individual boroughs or parishes, so it helps if you know which place is relevant to your ancestor. Use OHC's Heritage Search to locate records. Most are not available online, so you will need to visit the Centre to view documents. Holdings also include more than seventy oral history recordings, as well as photographs and obituaries, all accessible through Heritage Search and Picture Oxon.

PLACES TO VISIT

Soldiers of Oxfordshire Museum

The SOFO Museum tells the stories of the Oxfordshire regiments through thematic displays with information boards, uniforms, army vehicles and equipment, weapons, oral histories, interactive displays and other artefacts from the archives, plus a reconstruction of a

World War One trench. There is a changing programme of exhibitions, as well as regular talks and activities. www.sofo.org.uk

Imperial War Museum London

Opened in 1920 to demonstrate the bravery and sacrifice of troops during the First World War, the museum now captures the history and experience of conflict throughout the twentieth century. Exhibits include vehicles, tanks, planes, guns, uniforms and other artefacts. The Lord Ashcroft Gallery: Extraordinary Heroes, on Level 5, houses the world's largest collection of Victoria Crosses as well as George Crosses and other gallantry medals and tells the stories behind them. Included in the display are Oxfordshire soldiers Captain Noel Chavasse, the only double VC recipient during the First World War, and Corporal Alfred Wilcox of the Oxfordshire and Buckinghamshire Light Infantry. The museum has a well-stocked bookshop and a café. www.iwm.org.uk

FURTHER READING

General

Ashcroft, Michael, *Victoria Cross Heroes*, Headline Review, 2006
Ashcroft, Michael, *Victoria Cross Heroes Volume II*, Biteback Publishing, 2016
Ashcroft, Michael, *George Cross Heroes*, Headline Review, 2011
Clayton, Ann, *Chavasse – Double VC*, Pen & Sword Military, 2006
Fowler, Simon, *Researching Your Military Ancestors on the Internet*, Pen & Sword, 2007
Jenkins, Stanley C., *Oxfordshire at War Through Time*, Amberley Publishing, 2014

The Army

Fowler, Simon, *Tracing Your Army Ancestors*, Pen & Sword, 2006
Spencer, William, *Army Records: A Guide for Family Historians*, The National Archives, 2008

Oxfordshire Regiments

Crosse, Richard Banastre, *A Short History of the Oxfordshire and Buckinghamshire Light Infantry, 1741-1922*, Gale & Polden, 1925

Eddershaw, David, *The Story of The Oxfordshire Yeomanry 1798-1998*, Oxfordshire Yeomanry Trust, 1998

First World War

Fowler, Simon, *Tracing Your First World War Ancestors*, Countryside Books, 2008

Frampton, Bob, *Abingdon in the Great War*, Abingdon County Hall Museum, 2014

Graham, Malcolm, *Oxford in the Great War*, Pen & Sword, 2014

Second World War

Fowler, Simon, *Tracing Your Second World War Ancestors*, Countryside Books, 2006

Frampton, Bob, *Abingdon in World War II*, Abingdon County Hall Museum, 2016

Graham, Malcolm, *Oxfordshire at War 1939–45*, Sutton Publishing Ltd, 1994

Tomaselli, Phil, *Tracing Your Second World War Ancestors*, Pen & Sword, 2011

Royal Air Force

Spencer, William, *Air Force Records for Family Historians*, PRO Publications, 2000

Tomaselli, Phil, *Air Force Lives*, Pen & Sword, 2013

Tomaselli, Phil, *Tracing Your Air Force Ancestors*, Pen & Sword, 2014 (2nd edition)

Chapter 9

OXFORDSHIRE AT PLAY

THEATRE AND MUSIC

There is a long tradition of theatrical and musical entertainment in Oxfordshire – largely centred, unsurprisingly, in Oxford, which has been a hub for notable actors and musicians for over a hundred years. Shakespeare's company, the King's Men, performed in Oxford in the early seventeenth century, but would have been bound, like everyone else, by the university's ban on plays being performed in the city during term times – a restriction not lifted until the 1880s. Provincial theatres and concert halls began to appear in the early eighteenth century, and became increasingly popular during the nineteenth and twentieth centuries, giving a platform not only to professional performers but also to amateur performing groups.

Oxfordshire's theatres

Oxfordshire's oldest purpose-built theatre is the Kenton Theatre in Henley-on-Thames, which opened in 1805 and is the fourth oldest theatre in England (after the Old Vic in Bristol, the Theatre Royal in Richmond, Yorkshire, and the Theatre Royal in Margate). The theatre was commissioned by actors Sampson Penley and John Jonas and built on land that until 1790 was the site of a workhouse. Financial difficulties forced its closure in 1813, and for the next hundred years the theatre building was variously used as a non-conformist chapel, a Church of England school, a church hall and a storage facility.

Artist John Piper took over the lease in 1951 and redesigned the proscenium arch during a short period of closure. The theatre was dark again for five years from 1962, but re-opened in 1967 under the management of the Kenton Theatre Society and has remained in continuous operation since. The theatre is currently home to the Henley Amateur Operatic and Dramatic Society (formed 1922) and the Henley Players (formed 1948).

Oxford's New Theatre opened in St Mary's Hall Lane (now Oriel Street) in 1833, only to be replaced three years later by another theatre in Red Lion Yard, off George Street, which was known variously as the New Theatre, Victoria Theatre (or 'the Vic') and later the Theatre Royal. The theatre opened officially on Monday 4 July 1836 with a performance of *Much Ado About Nothing*. An announcement of the opening in *Jackson's Oxford Journal* (2 July 1836) tells us that prices ranged from 1s for the gallery to 3s 6d for the boxes, and that tickets had to be obtained from 'Mr Richard Stevens, fruiterer, Magdalen-street, near the Theatre'. Season tickets, costing £2 10s for the pit and £4 4s for the boxes, could be bought from 'Mr Barnett, at Mr. T. Randall's, hatter, High-street'.

The theatre closed in 1880 due to financial difficulties. With the support of Benjamin Jowett, the Master of Balliol, a company was set up to raise funds for a new theatre that could be used by local amateurs and university players as well as touring professionals. A new site in George Street was cleared for the new theatre, with eight businesses and private residences being demolished in the process.

The New Theatre Royal was designed by local architect H.G.W. Drinkwater and had a seating capacity of 1,000. It opened in February 1886 with a performance of *Twelfth Night* by the Oxford University Dramatic Society. The building was substantially altered in 1905, with the seating capacity being increased to 1,200.

In 1908, former box office clerk Charles Dorrill became manager, and the theatre was in the hands of the Dorrill family for the next sixty-four years. It was Charles's son, Stanley, who masterminded the building of the current theatre in the 1930s in a bid to create 'the most luxurious and comfortable house of entertainment in England'.

He commissioned theatre architects William and T.R. Milburn – whose portfolio included the Sunderland Empire, London's Dominion Theatre and the Glasgow Empire – to design the theatre, while the Art Deco interior was the handiwork of T.P. Bennett & Sons.

The New Theatre, its seating capacity increased to 1,710, had a grand opening on 26 February 1934. On 2 March, *The Oxford Times* reported:

> On every side of the auditorium could be seen people of distinction from city and university. The gathering had all the glamour of the first night in one of the famous West End theatres. It would be even truer to say that it recalled the scenes at continental opera houses.

Aladdin, the first pantomime at the New Theatre, 1934. © Oxfordshire County Council, Oxfordshire History Centre, Ref. POXO550601

For the next forty years, the Dorrills ensured a good mix of entertainment with opera, ballet, musical theatre, music hall, plays, concerts and comedy featured regularly, along with the annual pantomime. Some of the biggest names in the entertainment

The original Oxford Playhouse building in Woodstock Road was marked with a blue plaque in 2010 © Niola Lisle

industry trod the New Theatre's boards, including Des O'Connor, Danny La Rue, Lynsey de Paul and Alvin Stardust.

The Dorrill era came to an end in 1972 and the theatre had several changes of ownership over the next few years: Howard & Wyndham (1972–77), Apollo Leisure (1977–99); SFX (1999–2001); Clear Channel Entertainment (2001–05); Live Nation (2005–09) and Ambassador Theatre Group (2009–present). In 1977, Apollo Leisure changed the name to the Apollo Theatre – an unpopular decision locally – but it was changed back to the New Theatre by Clear Channel in 2003 after a major refurbishment.

In 1923, the New Theatre was joined by another theatre in the city, the Oxford Playhouse. Launched by London actress Jane Ellis, it was originally located in a former big game museum in Woodstock Road before moving to its current location in Beaumont Street in

1938. The new theatre was financed by Christ Church graduate Eric Dance, son of musical impresario Sir George Dance.

The Playhouse thrived during the war, becoming a good alternative venue for performers cast adrift by the closure of London's theatres. In 1956, new manager Frank Hauser established The Meadow Players as the resident professional company, while local groups such as the Oxford University Dramatic Society, Oxford University Experimental Theatre Club and Oxford Operatic Society also made their home here. From 1 January 1961, Oxford University took over the lease of the theatre, which was then billed as 'The University Theatre'.

The Oxford University Dramatic Society (OUDS), which was formed in 1885 by Alec MacKinnon, became one of the mainstays of the theatre, along with the Experimental Theatre Club (founded in 1936 by Nevill Coghill), the University College Players (formed 1941) and the Oxford Revue (founded 1952). Between them, these groups nurtured the talents of the likes of Rowan Atkinson, Hugh Grant, Dudley Moore, Maggie Smith, Mel Smith, Imogen Stubbs, Kenneth Tynan and Michael York. Diana Quick has the distinction of being the first female president of the OUDS, which didn't admit women until the 1960s.

In 1966, the Playhouse established the Burton Taylor Studio Theatre after Richard Burton and Elizabeth Taylor appeared in an OUDS production of *Dr Faustus* and provided funding towards a new intimate performance space for professional and amateur performers.

The second half of the twentieth century saw the emergence of a number of small theatres in Oxfordshire. The Unicorn Theatre in Abingdon is a tiny Elizabethan-style theatre created in 1952 by Alan Kitching, who converted the old Checkers Hall of the ruined Abingdon Abbey. It is now home to Abingdon Drama Club (founded 1944) and the Old Gaol Theatre Company (founded in the 1970s).

A derelict corn exchange in Wallingford was refurbished and opened in 1978 as a home for the Sinodun Players, a prominent amateur company established by former Gaiety Girl Frances Curtis in 1948. Agatha Christie, who lived locally, was President of the Sinodun Players from 1951 until her death in 1976. The Corn Exchange has featured as Causton Playhouse in *Midsomer Murders*.

The Theatre, Chipping Norton, opened in a former Salvation Army Citadel in December 1973, and puts on a wide variety of professional and amateur productions, while the Pegasus Theatre in Oxford opened in 1975 as a home for Oxford Youth Theatre (formed in 1962) and is a pioneering arts education space for young people.

Concert halls

The Holywell Music Room in central Oxford opened in 1748 and is Europe's oldest purpose-built concert hall. The idea for the Holywell is believed to have come from William Hayes, the university's Professor of Music. The building was designed by Thomas Camplin, the Vice-Principal of St Edmund Hall, and funded by public subscription. The Grade II-listed building is now part of the Oxford University's Faculty of Music, but hosts a variety of professional and amateur performers. It is now particularly associated with the Oxford Chamber Music Society, which was founded in 1898, and the Oxford Coffee Concerts series, established in 1986.

Sir Christopher Wren's Sheldonian Theatre, in Broad Street, was built in the late seventeenth century as the official ceremonial hall for the University of Oxford. It is still used as such, but is also a popular concert venue in the city, as is the Town Hall, which was built in 1897, primarily for municipal use. The Jaqueline du Pré Music Building opened in 1995, the first purpose-built concert hall in Oxford since the Holywell Music Room and now a venue for professional, amateur and student performers.

Finding theatre and music records

OHC holds the main archives for the Oxford Playhouse (O24 and O28) and its associated performing groups, including the Oxford University Dramatic Society. There are also records relating to other

The Holywell Music Room, Oxford, is Europe's oldest purpose-built concert hall
© Nicola Lisle

amateur societies, such as the Banbury and District Musical Society (O7) and the Oxford Bach Choir (O25), which was established in 1896 and is one of the county's longest-running amateur groups.

The Oxford Playhouse itself also holds a small archive of programmes from 1957–87, bound into volumes by year and arranged chronologically within each binder. These are not catalogued, so if you think your ancestor appeared at the Playhouse during this period it will save a lot of time if you know the relevant year. Programmes contain full lists of cast and creatives, but little in the way of biographical information. Many contain interesting articles about the history of the Playhouse. There are also some bound copies of *Theatre World* magazine for 1951. The March issue includes an article, 'Star-Spangled Oxford', by Godfrey Howard, which focuses on the history of the Playhouse, OUDS and the Experimental Theatre Club. The Playhouse archive is not generally open to the public, but can be viewed by appointment.

The archive for The Meadow Players is held by TAPC (www.vam.ac.uk/collections/theatre-performance) and covers its entire period of operation, 1956–74. Holdings include programmes, photographs, production files, designs and administrative papers. The TAPC also holds the Jack Keates Archive, which includes programmes, cuttings and posters relating to the New Theatre, Oxford, along with other provincial programmes from the nineteenth century to the 1970s. The London Pavilion Ltd/Variety Theatres Consolidated Archive holds material relating to music hall and variety acts in Britain, including Oxford. These archives can be accessed via the TAPC reading room by appointment.

The John Johnson Collection at the BOD includes playbills and programmes for Oxfordshire theatres and performing groups, including the New Theatre, Oxford Playhouse, The Meadow Players, OUDS and other college and amateur drama societies.

There is also a large amount of material relating to OUDS at the University of Bristol Theatre Collection (www.bristol.ac.uk/theatrecollection). Holdings include posters, press cuttings, programmes, leaflets, correspondence and photographs, as well as the papers of Professor Glynne Wickham, a leading light in OUDS and its first post-war president.

Regional papers such as *The Oxford Times*, *Oxford Mail* and *Jackson's Oxford Journal*, as well as the various university publications, are a good source for advertisements, reviews and obituaries, and can be found at the OHC and BOD. It is also worth checking out the BNA (www.britishnewspaperarchive.co.uk) for reviews and obituaries in specialist publications such as *The Stage* as well as the nationals.

Other good resources include the Association of Performing Arts Collections (www.performingartscollections.org.uk/resources), which has a searchable database of archives, and the TNA's guide to theatre, film and television archives (www.nationalarchives.gov.uk/help-with-your-research/research-guides/film-television-performing-arts-records-held-by-other-archives).

SPORT AND LEISURE

Sport has played a large part in Oxfordshire's social history. The university alone has a huge sporting heritage, producing countless champions such as Sir Roger Bannister, who ran the first sub-four-minute mile at Iffley Road in 1954, and Olympic rower Matthew Pinsent. But a variety of sports have also flourished throughout the county. Up to the late nineteenth century, the most popular sports were hunting, coursing, shooting, angling, racing and rowing. From around the 1880s, other sports began to appear as the Victorians embraced a variety of ball games including football, rugby, hockey, cricket, tennis and golf.

The oldest football club recognised by the Oxfordshire County Football Association is Henley Town FC, which was established in 1871 and has enjoyed championship success with various local leagues for much of its history. Another early club was Oxford City FC, which was founded in 1882 by George W. Gordon, a school teacher from Marlow, who served as the club's president from 1893–

1900. Oxford City FC enjoyed considerable success in its early days, but went into temporary decline during the mid-twentieth century. It bounced back in the 1990s and is still flourishing.

Meanwhile, another amateur side, Headington, formed in 1893, merged with Headington Quarry in 1911 to become Headington Utd. The club joined the senior league in 1921 and the Spartan League in 1947, turning professional in 1949 and changing its name to Oxford United in 1960.

The official Oxford United website has a detailed club history, an A-Z of players and match records. www.oufc.co.uk/club/history/

The OHC holds records for some of Oxfordshire's sports teams including Henley Golf Club (O13), Headington Ladies' Hockey Club (O198), Banbury Wanderers Athletic Club (O199) and East Oxford Bowls Club (O210).

There are also collections representing many of Oxfordshire's other leisure activities, including social clubs, village associations, women's institutes, townswomen's guilds and other societies, all within the O (Organisations) series. It is also worth searching newspapers for match reports, other sports and leisure news and obituaries. The photograph and oral history recordings also hold plenty of material relating to sports and leisure activities. The Museum of Oxford (www.museumofoxford.org) has displays relating to football and tennis.

Rowing

For a county with so much water at its disposal, it is hardly surprising that water sports have become popular. Rowing became a competitive sport during the early nineteenth century, with the first Oxford–Cambridge Boat Race taking place at Henley-on-Thames in 1829. The race began as a friendly challenge between former Harrovians Charles Wordsworth and Charles Merrivale, who went on to Oxford and Cambridge respectively but kept in touch and teased each other about the merits of their two universities. From this was born the idea of an inter-university boat race.

Regatta at Henley-on-Thames © Oxfordshire County Council, Oxfordshire HIstory Centre Ref. HT13309

The first encounter took place on 10 June 1829 between the newly-formed Oxford University Boat Club and the Cambridge University Boat Club (formed 1828). Although starting as the underdog, it was Oxford that prevailed – much to the dismay of punters who had reputedly placed bets of 500 guineas on a Cambridge victory.

This was the only time the race took place in Henley; the next race, in 1836, followed the professional scullers' course from Westminster to Putney, with the current route from Putney to Mortlake being established in 1845. The first Women's Boat Race took place in 1927, a year after the formation of the Oxford University Women's Boat Club (OUWBC), and became a permanent fixture in the 1960s despite initial hostility from their male counterparts.

Henley Royal Regatta started in 1839 as part of a single-day event with a fair and other entertainments, and quickly grew into a five-day competition that is now world famous. The event was given the 'Royal' title in 1851 when HRH Prince Albert became the regatta's first patron. Henley has acquired a number of local rowing clubs, including the Leander Club, which was established in London in 1818 and moved to Henley in 1897; others are Henley Rowing Club (founded 1839), the Upper Thames Rowing Club (founded 1963) and Henley Dragons (founded 1991).

To trace amateur rowing ancestors, the archive at the Henley River and Rowing Museum (www.rrm.co.uk) is a good place to start. Holdings include a set of Rowing Almanacs produced annually by the Amateur Rowing Association from 1865 to 2000. Each lists the result of races from the previous year and covers the Henley Royal Regatta and other regattas and races recorded by associated rowing clubs. There is no index of names, so it is essential to have some idea of which year(s) your ancestor raced.

Each race record includes dates, heats (with crew names, by initial and surname only), and sometimes race reports. Names of committee members, regatta secretaries and club secretaries are also included, as well as tables of winners, time records, statistics and crew listings with the weight of each crew member (probably the only place where you can find your ancestor's weight!). There is also general information such as qualification rules and general rules.

The early almanacs are tiny with very small print, but later issues were enlarged to A6 and then to A5. By 1959 almanacs included more detailed reviews, a few black and white photographs and the results of major races (such as the Boat Race and the Olympics) presented in tables for greater clarity.

The archive also has a large stock of regatta programmes from the Henley Town Council archive. These were issued daily throughout the regatta and can also contain information about your ancestors. The official Henley Royal Regatta programme for 7 July 1928, for example, includes lists of stewards, the management committee, umpires, judges and official timekeepers, along with a detailed list of races and crews racing that day.

The library and archive are open by appointment; alternatively, staff will undertake name searches for you. Additionally, if you have ancestors' trophies or plates with illegible inscriptions, archive staff might be able to help.

Archives relating to the Oxford University Boat Club are at the BOD (see Chapter 7). There are also holdings for various Oxford rowing clubs at the OHC (series O215).

MORRIS DANCING

Morris dancing in Oxfordshire dates back several hundred years, with different traditions developing in different villages. Many of the earlier Morris sides in Oxfordshire danced in the Cotswold tradition, but later on other traditions became popular.

Morris dancing was in decline during the nineteenth century, mainly as a result of the agricultural depression and the migration

Headington Quarry Morris Dancers, 1898 © Oxfordshire County Council, Oxfordshire History Centre, Ref. POX0104110

from villages to towns. Towards the end of the century, though, there was a revival, thanks largely to the efforts of people like folklore collector Percy Manning and Headington Morris dancer and accordionist William Kimber.

Manning's paper, *Oxfordshire's Seasonal Festivals*, published in 1897, included his extensive research on Morris dancing and helped to inspire a renewed interest. The Headington Quarry Morris Dancers were revived soon afterwards, after a decade of lying dormant. Before long, they caught the interest of the English folk song and dance revivalist Cecil Sharp, who invited William Kimber to help him preserve the dance steps and tunes for future generations. This sparked a widespread revival of Morris and other folk dancing in England, and led to the formation of the English Folk Dance and Song Society in London in 1932. Kimber began teaching Morris dancing at Headington Secondary School in 1945, thereby introducing a new generation to the tradition and ensuring its survival.

OHC has records for the Oxford City Morris Men (O35), which was founded in 1938. The collection includes correspondence and memoirs of past and current members, as well as a detailed history of the side. Use Heritage Search to find records related to other sides; you may find them mentioned in local newspapers or in oral history collections.

To find out more about the history of Morris dancing in Oxfordshire and current sides, visit www.oxfordshiremorris.org.

Percy Manning's research has been deposited at the BOD; you can access the collection at http://www.bodley.ox.ac.uk/dept/scwmss/wmss/online/modern/manning-percy/manning-percy.html.

PLACES TO VISIT

Museum of Oxford

Based in Oxford Town Hall, the museum has displays relating to the river and rowing, football, real tennis and other sports. www.museumofoxford.org

River & Rowing Museum, Henley-on-Thames © Nicola Lisle

River & Rowing Museum, Henley-on-Thames

This lovely riverside museum includes displays on the history of rowing on the Thames, the Henley Royal Regatta, the Oxford–Cambridge Boat Race and more, plus a changing programme of exhibitions. Café and shop. www.rrm.co.uk

FURTHER READING

Theatre and music

Carpenter, Humphrey, *OUDS: A Centenary History of the Oxford University Dramatic Society, 1885–1995*, OUP, 1985

Chapman, Don, *Oxford Playhouse: High and Low Drama in a University City*, University of Hertfordshire Press, 2008

Gascoigne, Bamber, *Cambridge History of the British Theatre*, CUP, 2004

Mee, John H., *The Oldest Music Room in Europe: A Record of Eighteenth Century Enterprise at Oxford*, Forgotten Books, 2015

Port, Bill, *The Well-Trod Stage*, Robinswood Press, 2005 [relates to the Kenton Theatre, Henley]
Ruston, Alan, *My Ancestor Worked in the Theatre*, Society of Genealogists, 2005
Stockwell, Alan, *Finding Sampson Penley*, Vesper Hawk, 2012

Sport and leisure

Bannister, Roger, *The First Four Minutes*, Sutton, 2004
Bolton, Geoffrey, *History of the OUCC (Oxford University Cricket Club)*, Holywell, 1962
Brodetsky, Martin, *Oxford United On This Day: History, Facts and Figures from Every Day of the Year*, Pitch Publishing Ltd, 2009
Brodetsky, Martin, *Oxford United Miscellany*, Pitch Publishing Ltd, 2010
Brodetsky, Martin, *Oxford United The Complete Record 1893-2009*, DB Publishing, 2012
Burnell, R.D., *The Oxford and Cambridge Boat Race, 1829–1953*, OUP, 1954
Burnell, Richard, *Henley Royal Regatta: A Celebration of 150 Years*, Heinemann, 1960
Dodd, Christopher, *Henley Royal Regatta*, Hutchinson, 1981
Dodd, Christopher and Marks, John, *Battle of the Blues: The Oxford and Cambridge Boat Race from 1829*, P to M Ltd, 2004
Macmichael, William Fisher, *The Oxford and Cambridge Boat Races: A Chronicle of the Contests on the Thames in Which University Crews Have Borne a Part, From AD 1829 to AD 1869, Compiled from the University Club Books and Other Contemporary and Authentic Records*, Forgotten Books, 2017
McCrery, Nigel, *Hear the Boat Sing: Oxford and Cambridge Rowers Killed in World War 1*, The History Press, 2017

Morris Dancing and folklore

Heaney, Mike (ed.), *Percy Manning, The Man Who Collected Oxfordshire*, Archaeopress, 2017

Chapter 10

DIRECTORY OF ARCHIVES, LIBRARIES AND OTHER USEFUL RESOURCES

This directory brings together all the archives, libraries, family history societies, museums, websites and other resources mentioned in the book, together with some additional ones that might be of interest, with full contact details. All details were correct at the time of publication, but it is advisable to check before visiting in case any have changed. Note that for most libraries and archives you will need a Reader's Ticket, for which requirements vary, so it is essential to check this before you visit. Many also require advance booking, so again it is essential to check on this.

GOVERNMENT ORGANISATIONS

General Register Office (England and Wales)
PO Box 2, Southport PR8 2JD
Tel: 0300 123 1837
Email: certificate.services@gro.gsi.gov.uk
Website: www.gov.uk/research-family-history

Principal Probate Registry
www.gov.uk/wills-probate-inheritance/searching-for-probate-records

NATIONAL ARCHIVES AND LIBRARIES

The British Library
96 Euston Road, London NW1 2DB
Tel: 0330 333 1144
Email: customer-services@bl.uk
www.bl.uk
Family history guide www.bl.uk/familyhistory.html

British Motor Industry Heritage Trust (BMIHT) Archive
British Motor Museum, Banbury Road, Gaydon, Warwickshire CV35 0BJ
Tel: 01926 641188
Email: enquiries@britishmotormuseum.co.uk
Website: www.britishmotormuseum.co.uk

Commonwealth War Graves Commission
2 Marlow Road, Maidenhead, Berkshire SL6 7DX
Tel; 01628 507200
Email: enquiries@cwgc.org
Website: www.cwgc.org

Dr Williams's Library (Congregational Collection)
Dr Williams's Trust, 14 Gordon Square, London WC1H 0AR
Tel: 020 7387 3727
Email: archives@dwl.ac.uk
Website: www.dwl.ac.uk

Methodist Archives and Research Centre (MARC)
The John Rylands Library, 150 Deansgate, Manchester M3 3EH
Tel: 0161 275 3764
Email: uml.special-collections@manchester.ac.uk
www.library.manchester.ac.uk/search-resources/guide-to-special-collections/methodist

Modern Records Centre
University Library, University of Warwick, Coventry CV4 7AL
Tel: 0247 652 4219
Email: archives@warwick.ac.uk
Website:
http://www2.warwick.ac.uk/services/library/mrc/holdings/main_archives

The National Archives
Kew, Richmond, Surrey TW9 4DU
Tel: 020 8876 3444
Email: online contact form
www.nationalarchives.gov.uk

Parliamentary Archives
Houses of Parliament, London SW1A 0PW
Tel: 020 7219 3074
Email: archives@parliament.uk
Website: www.parliament.uk/business/publications/parliamentary-archives/explore-guides-to-documentary-archive-/familyhistory/

Royal College of Nursing Library and Heritage Centre
20 Cavendish Square, London W1G 0RN
Tel: 020 7409 3333
Email: rcn.library@rcn.org.uk
Website: www.rcn.org.uk/library/services/family-history

Royal College of Surgeons Archives
35-43 Lincoln's Inn Fields, London WC2A 3PE
Tel: 020 7405 3474
Email: archives@rcseng.ac.uk
Website: www.rcseng.ac.uk/museums-and-archives/archives

Royal College of Physicians
11 St Andrews Place, Regent's Park, London NW1 4LE
Tel: 020 3075 1543
Email: history@rcplondon.ac.uk
Website: www.rcplondon.ac.uk/archive-and-historical-library-collections

Society of Genealogists
14 Charterhouse Buildings, Goswell Road, London EC1M 7BA
Tel: 020 7251 8799
Email: genealogy@sog.org.uk
Website: www.sog.org.uk

University of Bristol Theatre Archive
Faculty of Arts, Vandyck Building, 21 Park Row, Bristol BS1 5LT
Tel: 0117 331 5045
Email: theatre-collection@bristol.ac.uk
www.bristol.ac.uk/theatrecollection

Victoria & Albert Museum Theatre and Performance Collection
Blythe House, 23 Blythe Road, London W14 0QX
Tel: 020 7942 2698
Email: tmenquiries@vam.ac.uk.
https://www.vam.ac.uk/collections/theatre-performance

The Wellcome Library
183 Euston Road, London NW1 2BE
Tel: 020 7611 8722
Email: library@wellcome.ac.uk
https://wellcomelibrary.org/

LOCAL ARCHIVES AND LIBRARIES

The Angus Library and Archive

Leading collection of Baptist history and heritage worldwide.
Regent's Park College, Pusey Street, Oxford OX1 2LB
Tel: 01855 288120
Email: angus.library@regents.ox.ac.uk
Website: http://theangus.rpc.ox.ac.uk

Bodleian Library Special Collections

Deposited papers relating to individuals, university clubs and societies, plus some records related to the city of Oxford.
Weston Library, Broad Street, Oxford OX1 3BG
Tel: 01865 277150
Email: specialcollections.enquiries@bodleian.ox.ac.uk
Website: www.bodleian.ox.ac.uk/weston

Centre for Buckinghamshire Studies

County Hall, Walton Street, Aylesbury, Buckinghamshire HP20 1UA
Tel: 01296 395000
Email: archives@buckscc.gov.uk
Website: www.buckscc.gov.uk

John Johnson Collection (part of Bodleian Library Special Collections)

One of the world's largest collections of printed ephemera.
Weston Library, Broad Street, Oxford OX1 3BG
Tel: 01865 277150
Email: specialcollections.enquiries@bodleian.ox.ac.uk
Website: www.bodleian.ox.ac.uk/johnson

Leicestershire County Council (Family History)

County Hall, Glenfield, Leicestershire LE3 8RA
Tel: 0116 232 3232
www.leicestershire.gov.uk/registrars/trace-your-family-tree/researching-your-family-history

Oxford Brookes University Special Collections
Includes the Oxford Brookes University Collection, National Brewing Library and Wesley Historical Society Library.
Oxford Brookes University, Headington Road, Oxford OX3 0BP
Tel: 01865 484130
www.brookes.ac.uk/library/special-collections

Oxford University Archives
Administrative records of the university from 1214; includes student matriculation, examination and graduation records. Website includes history of the university and information about awarding degrees.
Bodleian Library, Broad Street, Oxford OX1 3BG
Tel: 01865 277145
Email: enquiries@oua.ox.ac.uk
Website: www.bodleian.ox.ac.uk/oua

Oxford University Press Archives
Detailed records of OUP staff, clubs and societies from the First World War onwards. Adjacent museum tells the story of the OUP and includes old printing equipment.
Great Clarendon Street, Oxford OX2 6DP
Tel: 01865 353527
Email: archives@oup.com
https://global.oup.com/uk/archives/index.html

Oxfordshire County Library
Queen Street, Westgate, Oxford OX1 1DJ
Tel: 01865 815509
www.oxfordshire.gov.uk/cms/public-site/libraries
For details of all Oxfordshire county libraries, visit www.oxfordshire. gov.uk/cms/public-site/find-library

Oxfordshire Health Archives
Oxfordshire History Centre, St Luke's Church, Temple Road, Oxford OX4 2HT

Telephone: 01865 398243
Email: archives@oxfordhealth.nhs.uk
www.oxfordshirehealtharchives.nhs.uk

Oxfordshire History Centre
St Luke's Church, Temple Road, Oxford OX4 2HT
Telephone: 01865 398200
Email: oxhist@oxfordshire.gov.uk
www.oxfordshire.gov.uk/cms/public-site/oxfordshire-history-centre

Trinity College Dublin
Manuscripts and Archives Research Library
Trinity College, College Street, Dublin 2, Ireland
Tel: 0353 1 896 1189
Email: mscripts@tcd.ie
www.tcd.ie/library/manuscripts/index.php

MUSEUMS, HERITAGE CENTRES AND OTHER PLACES OF HISTORIC INTEREST

Oxfordshire

Abingdon County Hall Museum
Permanent displays on the history of the town, including artefacts related to the MG factory and the town's canal, railway and brewing heritage, as well as a 'town treasures' exhibition and changing exhibitions in a Grade I listed building. Café and shop.
Market Place, Abingdon, Oxon OX14 3HG
Tel: 01235 523703
abingdon.museum@abingdon.gov.uk
www.abingdon.gov.uk/partners/abingdon-county-hall-museum

Ashmolean Museum
The oldest public museum in the world, featuring galleries devoted to local and global art, culture, history and archaeology. Regular events, activities and changing exhibitions. Shop, café and rooftop restaurant.

Beaumont Street, Oxford OX1 2PH
Tel: 01865 278000
www.ashmolean.org

Bampton Community Archive
Extensive collection of photographs, press cuttings, documents, sound and video files exploring Bampton's social history and customs. Searchable database (including online). Regular exhibitions.
The Old Grammar School, Church View, Bampton OX18 2HA
Tel: 01993 851041
Email: info@thecoachhousebampton.co.uk
http://bamptonarchive.org

Banbury Museum
Castle Quay Shopping Centre, Spiceball Park Road, Banbury, Oxon OX16 2PQ
Tel: 01295 753752
Email: enquiries@banburymuseum.org
www.banburymuseum.org

Blenheim Palace
Woodstock, Oxfordshire OX20 1PS
Tel: 01993 810530
Email: customerservice@blenheimpalace.com
www.blenheimpalace.com

Bloxham Village Museum
Church Street, Bloxham, Banbury OX15 4ET
Tel: 07721 187813
Email: bloxham.museum@gmail.com
www.bloxhammuseum.com

British Motor Museum
Banbury Road, Gaydon, Warwickshire CV35 0BJ
Tel: 01926 641188

Email: enquiries@britishmotormuseum.co.uk
www.britishmotormuseum.co.uk

Broughton Castle
Fourteenth-century moated manor house that became a meeting place for Parliamentarians until it was besieged by the Royalist troops in 1642.
Banbury, Oxfordshire OX15 5EB
Tel: 01295 276070
Email: info@broughtoncastle.com
www.broughtoncastle.com

Charlbury Museum
Displays relating to local crafts and industries, and large archive of maps and photographs illustrating day-to-day life and local events.
Market Street, Charlbury OX7 3PN
Tel: 01608 810656/810709
www.charlbury.info/community/42

Chastleton House (National Trust)
Former wool merchant's house dating from the seventeenth century, which has changed little over 400 years.
Chastleton, Nr Moreton-in-Marsh GL56 0SU
Tel: 01494 755560
www.nationaltrust.org.uk/chastleton

Chipping Norton Museum of Local History
Run by the Chipping Norton History Society. Displays relating to local wool, brewing, farming and iron founding industries. Local Study Centre with extensive collection of local family history records on microfiche.
4 High Street, Chipping Norton, Oxon OX7 5AD
Tel: 01608 641712
www.chippingnortonmuseum.org.uk

Churchill & Sarsden Heritage Centre
Based in a restored medieval church; local history displays plus focus on famous men of the village, including 'father of geology' William Smith. Good selection of local family history resources, including census records, wills, family trees and memorial, burial and baptism registers. Changing exhibitions.
Hastings Hill, Churchill, Nr. Chipping Norton, OX7 6NA
Tel: 01608 658603
Email: churchillheritage@gmail.com
www.churchillheritage.org.uk

Cogges Manor Farm Museum
Over 1,000 years of history at a Cotswold manor and farm buildings, parts of which date back to the thirteenth century; at one time the home of the Blake family of wool merchants. Regular activities and exhibitions. Shop and café.
Church Lane, Witney, Oxon OX28 3LA
Tel: 01993 772602
www.cogges.org.uk

Combe Mill
Victorian sawmill with working steam engine, waterwheel and blacksmith's forge. Regular steam days and other events. Shop and riverside café.
Blenheim Palace Sawmills, Combe OX29 8ET
Tel: 01993 358694
www.combemill.org

Didcot Railway Centre
Collection of GWR steam engines, coaches, wagons and other relics, plus original 1932 engine shed. Museum with artefacts and memorabilia from the 1830s, large photographic collection and archive. Regular steam days and other events. Shop, café and picnic area.
Didcot OX11 7NJ
Tel: 01235 817200

Email: info@didcotrailwaycentre.org.uk
www.didcotrailwaycentre.org.uk

Dorchester Abbey Museum
High Street, Dorchester-on-Thames, Wallingford, Oxon OX10 7HH
Email: museum@dorchester-abbey.org.uk
www.dorchester-abbey.org.uk/museum.htm

Hook Norton Brewery Museum and Village Museum
Brewery Lane, Hook Norton, Banbury OX15 5NY
Tel: 01608 730384
Email: heritage@hook-norton-brewery.co.uk
www.hooky.co.uk

Kelmscott Manor
Former home of poet, designer and craftsman William Morris. Shop and tea room.
Kelmscott, Lechlade GL7 3HJ
Tel: 01367 252486
Email: admin@kelmscottmanor.org.uk
www.kelmscottmanor.org.uk

The MG Car Club
Founded 1930; its headquarters now has an MG exhibition, library, photograph archive and production manuals, plus a small shop.
Kimber House, 12 Cemetery Road, Abingdon OX14 1AS
Tel: 01235 555552
Email: mgcc@mgcc.co.uk
www.mgcc.co.uk

Mini Plant Oxford
Eastern Bypass Road, Cowley, Oxford OX4 6NL
Tel: 01865 825750
Email: info@visit.mini.com
www.visitmini.com

Museum of the History of Science
Extensive collection of scientific instruments housed in the original Ashmolean Museum building, the oldest purpose-built public museum building in the world. Regular lectures, gallery tours and other events.
Broad Street, Oxford OX1 3AZ
Tel: 01865 277280
Email: museum@mhs.ox.ac.uk
www.mhs.ox.ac.uk

Museum of Oxford
The story of Oxford and the University told through a range of artefacts and interactive displays. The museum is currently being redeveloped and is expected to be fully open in 2020. Meanwhile, there are displays in two Explore Oxford galleries, as well as regular exhibitions, workshops, talks and other activities in the museum and the nearby Heritage Learning Centre. Small shop and café.
Oxford Town Hall, St Aldates, Oxford OX1 1BZ
Tel: 01865 252334 (gift shop)
Email: museum@oxford.gov.uk
www.museumofoxford.org

Nuffield Place
Huntercombe, Henley-on-Thames RG9 5RY
Tel: 01491 641224
Email: nuffieldplace@nationaltrust.org.uk
www.nationaltrust.org.uk/nuffield-place

Oxford Botanic Garden
Oxford University's historic botanic garden, founded in 1621 and now home to around 5000 plant species from around the world. Riverside walk and views of the dreaming spires.
Rose Lane, Oxford OX1 4AZ
Tel: 01865 286690
www.botanic-garden.ox.ac.uk

Oxford Bus Museum and Morris Motors Museum
Station Yard, Long Hanborough, Witney OX29 8LA
Tel: 01993 883617
www.oxfordbusmuseum.org.uk

Oxford Castle Unlocked
The story of the eleventh-century castle, which served as a prison until 1996. Guided tours only. Shop, café and restaurants.
44-46 Oxford Castle, Oxford OX1 1AY
Tel: 01865 260666
Email: info@oxfordcastleunlocked.co.uk
www.oxfordcastleunlocked.co.uk

Oxford University Museum of Natural History
Founded in 1860; now an internationally-important collection of geological and zoological artefacts, plus large archive and library for scientific research. Regular events. Shop.
Parks Road, Oxford OX1 3PW
Tel: 01865 272950
Email: info@oum.ox.ac.uk
www.oum.ox.ac.uk

Oxfordshire Museum
Displays relating to local history, with a focus on Anglo-Saxon, Roman and Victorian Oxfordshire. Also art, countryside and landscape. Dinosaur garden, café and shop. Regular events.
Fletcher's House, Park Street, Woodstock OX20 1SN
Tel: 01993 814106
Email: oxon.museum@oxfordshire.gov.uk
www.oxfordshire.gov.uk/oxfordshiremuseum

Oxfordshire Museums Resource Centre
Collection of objects and pictures relating to Oxfordshire archaeology and history. Access by appointment.

Cotswold Dene, Standlake OX29 7QG
Tel: 01865 300972
Email: museums.resource.centre@oxfordshire.gov.uk
www.mrc-occ.org.uk

Pendon Museum
Model railway capturing the Vale of White Horse in the 1920s and 1930s. Shop and regular events.
Long Wittenham, Abingdon OX14 4QD
Tel: 01865 407365
Email: info@pendonmuseum.com
www.pendonmuseum.com

Pitt Rivers Museum
Founded 1884; world-famous display of everyday objects from around the world.
South Parks Road, Oxford OX1 3PP
Tel: 01865 270927
Email: prm@prm.ox.ac.uk
www.prm.ox.ac.uk

River & Rowing Museum
Mill Meadows, Henley-on-Thames, Oxon RG9 1BF
Tel: 01491 415600
Email: curatorial@rrm.co.uk (for library/archive research)
www.rrm.co.uk

Shrivenham Heritage Society
Large collection of documents, maps, photographs, censuses and old Parish Council records. Searchable online catalogue.
Memorial Hall, Highworth Road, Shrivenham SN6 8DZ
Tel: 01793 782748
Email: info@shrivenhamheritagesociety.co.uk
www.shrivenhamheritagesociety.co.uk

Soldiers of Oxfordshire Trust Museum and Archives
Park Street, Woodstock, Oxfordshire OX20 1SN
Tel: 01993 810215 (Collections & Research)
Email: collections@sofo.org.uk
www.sofo.org.uk

Stonor Park
Henley-on-Thames, Oxfordshire RG9 6HF
Tel: 01491 638587
Email: enquiries@stonor.com
Website: www.stonor.com

Swalcliffe Barn
Old agricultural and trade vehicles on display in a fifteenth century barn.
Shipston Road, Swalcliffe, Banbury OX15 5DR
Tel: 01295 788278
Email: jcdemmar@btinternet.com
www.culture24.org.uk/am31904

Swinford Museum
Collection of local domestic, agricultural, trade and craft objects capturing a bygone rural community. Changing exhibitions.
Filkins, Lechlade GL7 3JW
Tel: 01367 860504
http://filkins.org.uk/village-facilities/swinford-museum/

Thame Museum
Local history displays, plus a refurbished room belonging to an Elizabethan merchant from Thame. Monthly talks and changing exhibitions.
79 High Street, Thame OX9 3AE
Tel: 01844 212801
Email: info@thamemuseum.org
www.thamemuseum.org

Thames Valley Police Museum
Sulhamstead House, Sulhamstead, Reading RG7 4DU
Tel: 01865 542704
Email: TVPMuseum@thamesvalley.pnn.police.uk
Website: www.thamesvalley.police.uk/about-us/who-we-are/ thames-valley-police-museum
At the time of writing, Sulhamstead House is closed for refurbishment and the museum is being moved to temporary accommodation in Theale, near Reading. The refurbishment is expected to take 12-24 months to complete. Check the website for updates.

Tolsey Museum
Tools from local crafts and trades, locally-stitched samplers, seventeenth century trade tokens, Corporation documents, Maces and seals, dolls' house and large photographic collection.
Email: tolseymuseum@yahoo.co.uk
126 High Street, Burford OX18 4QU
www.tolseymuseumburford.org

Tom Brown's School Museum
Housed in the seventeenth-century schoolroom that featured in *Tom Brown's Schooldays* by local author Thomas Hughes. History of Uffington told through artefacts, documents, photographs, oral history recordings, press cuttings, census records and more. Displays relating to Thomas Hughes and John Betjeman. Changing exhibitions. Books for sale.
Broad Street, Uffington SN7 7RA
Tel: 01367 820978
Email: museum@uffington.net
www.museum.uffington.net

Tooley's Boatyard
Banbury Museum, Spiceball Park Road, Banbury OX16 2PQ
Tel: 01295 272917

Email: info@tooleysboatyard.co.uk
www.tooleysboatyard.co.uk

Vale & Downland Museum
19 Church Street, Wantage OX12 8BL
Tel: 01235 771447
Email: vale.downland@gmail.com
www.wantage-museum.com

Wallingford Castle
The ruined remains of Wallingford Castle are now Grade 1 listed and are part of Castle Meadows, an important wildlife area managed by Earth Trust. Entrance is free.
Castle Street, Wallingford, Oxfordshire OD10 0BW
Earth Trust can be contacted at Little Wittenham, Oxfordshire OX14 4QZ
Tel: 01865 407792
Email: admin@earthtrust.org.uk
www.earthtrust.org.uk

Wallingford Museum
Interactive telling of the story of Wallingford with a Victorian street scene, River Thames displays, Agatha Christie exhibition and more. Regular events, changing exhibitions and guided town walks. Shop.
Flint House, 52 High Street, Wallingford OX10 0DB
Tel: 01491 835065
Email: admin@wallingfordmuseum.org.uk
www.wallingfordmuseum.org.uk

Waterperry Rural Life Museum
Waterperry Gardens, Waterperry, Nr Wheatley OX33 1JZ
Tel: 01844 339254
Email: office@waterperrygardens.co.uk
www.waterperrygardens.co.uk

The Witney Blanket Hall
100 High Street, Witney OX28 6HL
Tel: 01993 706408
Email: eleanor@blankethall.co.uk
www.cotswoldwoollenweavers.co.uk/blankethall.html

Witney and District Museum
Gloucester Court Mews, 75 High Street, Witney, Oxon OX28 6JA
Tel: 01993 775915
Email: contact@witneyhistory.org
Website: www.witneyhistory.org/witneymuseum.html

Wychwood Brewery
Eagle Maltings, The Crofts, Witney, Oxon OX28 4DP
Tel: 01993 890800
www.wychwood.co.uk

Further afield

Imperial War Museum
Displays and archives relating to conflicts from the First World War onwards. Includes the Lord Ashcroft Gallery of medals. Café and shop. Entrance is free.
Lambeth Road, London SE1 6HZ
Tel: 020 7416 5000
Website: www.iwm.org.uk

The Museum of English Rural Life
University of Reading, Redlands Road, Reading RG1 5EX
Tel: 0118 378 8660
Email: merl@reading.ac.uk
https://merl.reading.ac.uk

National Army Museum
Displays and archives relating to the British Army from the seventeenth century.
Royal Hospital Road, Chelsea, London SW3 4HT
Tel:
Website: www.nam.ac.uk

National Museum of the Royal Navy
HM Naval Base (PP66), Portsmouth PO1 3NH
Tel: 02392 891370
Email: library@nmrn.org.uk
www.nmrn.org.uk

National Railway Museum Library & Archive
Leeman Road, York YO26 4XJ
Tel: 08448 153139
Email: nrm.visitorservices@nrm.org.uk or use online form
Website: www.nrm.org.uk

Royal Air Force Museum and Archives
Grahame Park Way, London NW9 5LL
Tel: 020 8205 2266
Email: london@rafmuseum.org
Website: www.rafmuseum.org.uk/london

Royal Green Jackets (Rifles) Museum
Displays relating to the history of the Royal Green Jackets and its antecedent regiments, including the Oxfordshire and Buckinghamshire Light Infantry. Shop and café.
Peninsula Barracks, Romsey Road, Winchester, Hants SO23 8TS
Tel: 01962 828549
Email: archives@rgjmuseum.co.uk
Website: http://rgjmuseum.co.uk

FAMILY AND LOCAL HISTORY SOCIETIES

The Association of Genealogists and Researchers in Archives (AGRA)
Email: info@agra.org.uk
Website: www.agra.org.uk

Berkshire Record Society
Publishes scholarly editions of documents relating to Berkshire history, including thc area now in Oxfordshire.
c/o Berkshire Record Office, 9 Coley Avenue, Reading, Berkshire RG1 6AF
www.berkshirerecordsociety.org.uk

Berkshire Family History Society
The Centre for Heritage and Family History, 2nd Floor, Reading Central Library, Abbey Square, Reading, Berks RG1 3BQ
Tel: 0118 950 9553
Email: centre@berksfhs.org.uk
Website: www.berksfhs.org.uk

British Association for Local History
Promotes the study of local history. Visit the website for news, resources and publications.
BALH Head Office, Chester House, 68 Chestergate, Macclesfield SK11 6DY
Tel: 01625 664524
Email: Online enquiry form
www.balh.org.uk

Catholic Family History Society
Email: cfhsrecords@gmail.com
Website: www.catholicfhs.co.uk

The Catholic Record Society
Founded in 1904; has produced a wide range of publications relating to Catholic history and genealogy. Their Records series, which consists of transcripts of original documents, is of particular use to family historians.
Online contact form.
www.catholicrecordsociety.co.uk

Federation of Family History Societies
Articles, courses, resources and research tips.
PO Box 62 Sheringham NR26 9AR
Tel: 0800 0856322
Email: info@ffhs.org.uk
Website: www.ffhs.org.uk

Institute of Heraldic and Genealogical Studies
Email: registrar@ihgs.ac.uk
Website: www.ihgs.ac.uk

Jewish Genealogical Society of Great Britain
Email: secretary@jgsb.org.uk
Website: www.jgsgb.org.uk

Oxfordshire Family History Society
Founded 1976; holds monthly talks, helpdesks at local libraries and an annual history fair, and produces its own journal, *Oxfordshire Family Historian.* Transcripts of parish registers, monumental inscriptions, censuses and quarter sessions available for purchase.
Helpline: 01865 358151 or email help@ofhs.org.uk
www.ofhs.org.uk

Oxfordshire Local History Association
Excellent resource for variety of local history topics and issues relating to Oxfordshire and old Berkshire. News of local talks, exhibitions, guided walks, study days and other events, plus directory

of local history societies in Oxfordshire.
www.olha.org.uk

Oxfordshire Record Society
Publishes transcripts, abstracts and lists of primary sources relating to the history of Oxfordshire.
Email: oxfordshirerecordsociety@gmail.com
Website: www.oxfordshire-record-society.org.uk/index.htm

Quaker Family History Society
Email: info@qfhs.co.uk
Website: www.afhs.co.uk

USEFUL WEBSITES

Association of Performing Arts Collections (APAC)
www.performingartscollections.org.uk/resources
(Search UK Theatre Collections)

Baptist Historical Society
http://baptisthistory.org.uk/discover/family-history

BBC History
Covers a wide variety of events and topics.
www.bbc.co.uk/history

The Brewery History Society
www.breweryhistory.com

British Newspaper Archive
www.britishnewspaperarchive.co.uk

Cyndi's List
A comprehensive list of online family history resources.
www.cyndislist.com

Deceased Online
Central database for UK burials and cremations
www.deceasedonline.com

Family Search
The world's largest collection of free family history records, provided by the Church of Jesus Christ of Latter-Day Saints.
www.familysearch.org

Family Relatives
Comprehensive set of searchable records; some free to view, others are pay per view or subscription only
www.familyrelatives.com

Find a Grave
www.findagrave.com

Free BMD
Free search of birth, marriage and death records for England and Wales
www.freebmd.org.uk

Free Cen
Free search of the censuses
www.freecen.org.uk

Free Reg
Free search of parish registers
www.freereg.org.uk

The Gen Guide
Excellent resource for family historians. Lots of useful sources, advice, contacts and links.
www.genguide.co.uk

Genuki Berkshire
www.genuki.org.uk/big/eng/BRK

Genuki Oxfordshire
www.genuki.org.uk/big/eng/OXF

Jim Shead's Waterways Information
Comprehensive guide to the history of inland waterways in Britain.
www.jim-shead.com/waterways/index.php

Lord Ashcroft Medal Collection
Background to the collection and lists of recipients by name, conflict, date gazetted and service.
www.lordashcroftmedals.com

Our Criminal Ancestors
History of crime, punishment, police and the courts in England, plus family history tips.
www.ourcriminalancestors.org

Oxford Canal Heritage Trust
www.oxfordcanalheritage.org

Oxford History
www.oxfordhistory.org.uk

Oxfordshire Migrant/Emigration Lists and Records
http://www.ukgdl.org.uk/county/oxfordshire/migrant_lists

Oxfordshire Record Society
www.oxfordshire-record-society.org.uk

UK BMD
Transcriptions for UK births, marriages, deaths, census returns and other records.
www.ukbmd.org.uk

Victoria County History
A vast encyclopaedic record of England's people and places, founded in 1899 and based at the University of London's Institute of Historical Research since 1933. Plenty of material relating to the history of Oxfordshire.
www.victoriacountyhistory.ac.uk

Virtual Genealogical Society
Launched in April 2018 to provide an online forum for family historians with opportunities for networking, mentoring, taking part in webinars, attending conferences and other events, and much more.
https://virtualgensoc.com

WikiTree
Collaborate online project to create a worldwide family tree. Search free for your ancestors; results will give you birth, marriage and death dates, names of parents, siblings and spouse, and links to further records.
www.wikitree.com

Witney Blanket Story
www.witneyblanketstory.org.uk/wbp.asp

Workhouses
History of all aspects of workhouses, migration and immigration, and Poor Laws.
www.workhouses.org.uk

FAMILY HISTORY MAILING LISTS AND ONLINE FORUMS

Curious Fox
www.curiousfox.com/uk/r.lasso?vid=70074

Rootsweb
http://lists.rootsweb.ancestry.com/index/intl/ENG/OXFORDSHIRE.html

INDEX